SCHOLASTIC

BOOK OF WORLD RECORDS 2007

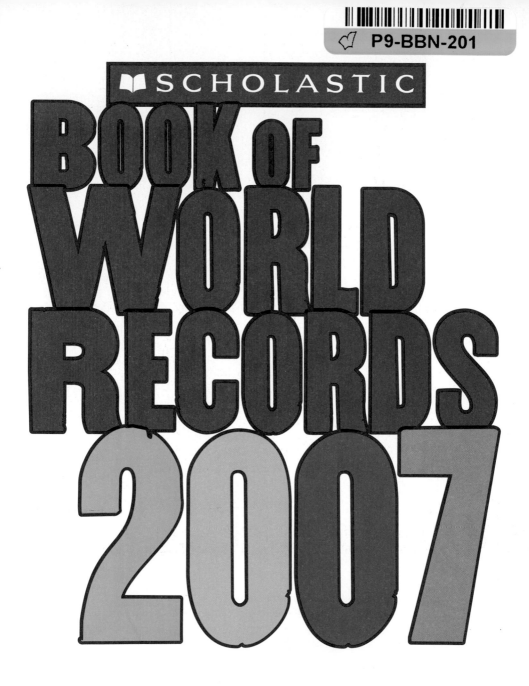

by Jenifer Corr Morse

A GEORGIAN BAY BOOK

SCHOLASTIC REFERENCE

To Isabelle Nicole—May you always find wonder in the world.
–JCM

CREATED AND PRODUCED BY GEORGIAN BAY ASSOCIATES, LLC

Georgian Bay Staff
Bruce S. Glassman, Executive Editor
Jenifer Corr Morse, Photo Editor
Calico Harington, Design

Scholastic Reference Staff
Andrea Pinkney, Vice President and Publisher
Mary Varilla Jones, Senior Editor
Brenda Murray, Assistant Editor
Becky Terhune, Art Director
Tatiana Sperhacke, Designer
Dwayne Howard, Photo Researcher

In most cases, the graphs in this book represent the top five record holders in each category.
However, in some graphs, we have chosen to list well-known or common people, places,
animals, or things that will help you better understand how extraordinary the record holder
is. These may not be the top five in the category. Additionally, some graphs have fewer than
five entries because so few people or objects reflect the necessary criteria.

ISBN-13: 978-0-545-00333-9
ISBN-10: 0-545-00333-4

10 9 8 7 6 5 4 3 2   7 8 9 10 11/0
Printed in the U.S.A.   23
This edition first printing, January 2007

CONTENTS

Sports Records   5

Track and Field 6
Bicycling 7
Golf 8
Basketball 12
Baseball. 22
Football. 35
Tennis 44
Figure Skating. 48
Olympics 50
Soccer. 58
Hockey 62
Car Racing 66

Human-Made Records   69

Transportation 70
Constructions 74
Travel 86

Nature Records   91

Animals 92
Natural Formations 124
Food 136
Weather 145
Plants 151
Disasters 160

Popular Culture Records 166

Television. 167
Music. 171
Theater 180
Movies. 182
Books 193
Art 194

Money and Business Records 195

Industry. 196
Wealth. 202
Most Valuable 207

Science Records 213

Computers 214
Technology. 219
Solar System. 223
Space 233
Video Games. 235
Vehicles 236

U.S. Records 245

Index. 296

Sports Records

Track and Field • Bicycling • Golf • Basketball
Baseball • Football • Tennis • Figure Skating
Olympics • Soccer • Hockey • Car Racing

Runner with the
World's Fastest Mile

Hicham El Guerrouj

Runners with the
WORLD'S FASTEST MILE

Time in minutes and seconds

3:43.13	3:43.40	3:44.39	3:44.60	3:44.90
Hicham El Guerrouj, Morocco	Noah Ngeny, Kenya	Noureddine Morceli, Algeria	Hicham El Guerrouj, Morocco	Hicham El Guerrouj, Morocco

Moroccan runner Hicham El Guerrouj is super speedy—he ran a mile in just over 3 minutes and 43 seconds in July 1999 while racing in Rome. He also holds the record for the fastest mile in North America with a time just short of 3 minutes and 50 seconds. El Guerrouj is also an Olympian with gold medals in the 1500-meter and 5000-meter races. With this accomplishment at the 2004 Athens Games, he became the first runner to win both races at the same Olympics in more than 75 years. El Guerrouj returned to the Olympics in 2006 as a torchbearer in Torino, Italy.

Cyclist with the
Most Tour de France Wins

Lance Armstrong

Lance Armstrong was the first cyclist to cross the finish line to win seven Tour de France races. Armstrong won his first race in 1999, just three years after being diagnosed with cancer. He went on to win the top cycling event for the next six years, retiring after his 2005 victory. Armstrong has received many awards and honors during his career, including being named *Sports Illustrated*'s "Sportsman of the Year" in 2002. Armstrong also formed the Lance Armstrong Foundation that supports people recovering from cancer.

Cyclists with the
MOST TOUR DE FRANCE WINS

Number of first-place finishes

Lance Armstrong, USA	Eddy Merckx, Belgium	Jacques Anquetil, France	Bernard Hinault, France	Miguel Indurain, Spain
7	5	5	5	5

LPGA Golfer with the Lowest Seasonal Average

Annika Sorenstam

With an average of 69.33, Swedish golfer Annika Sorenstam had the lowest seasonal average in the LPGA in 2005. Sorenstam began her professional career in 1994 and has set or tied 30 LPGA records since then. In 2002, she became the first female player to finish below 69.0 with an average of 68.7. Sorenstam was born in Stockholm in 1970 and began playing golf at age 12. In 2003, Sorenstam became the first woman in 58 years to compete in a PGA event when she played in the Bank of America Colonial tournament.

LPGA Golfers with the
LOWEST SEASONAL AVERAGES

Seasonal average in 2005

Annika Sorenstam	Cristie Kerr	Paula Creamer	Jeong Jang	Natalie Gulbis
69.33	70.86	70.98	71.17	71.24

PGA Player with the
Lowest Seasonal Average

Tiger Woods

Tiger Woods was at the top of his game in 2005 with the lowest PGA seasonal average of 68.66. Woods started his professional golfing career in 1996, and since then he has won more than 65 tournaments. Woods also helped the United States win the World Cup team title in 2000. And at 21 years old, he became the youngest person to complete the career Grand Slam of professional major championships that same year. In 2001, he became the first golfer in history to hold all four professional major championships at the same time. Wood's worldwide career winnings total more than $68.1 million.

PGA Players with the
LOWEST SEASONAL AVERAGES

Seasonal average in 2005

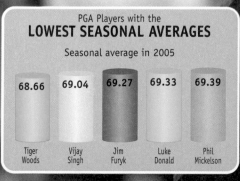

68.66	69.04	69.27	69.33	69.39
Tiger Woods	Vijay Singh	Jim Furyk	Luke Donald	Phil Mickelson

The LPGA's
Highest-Paid Golfer

Annika Sorenstam

Annika Sorenstam has earned $18.6 million since her LPGA career began in 1994. During this time, she has had 66 career victories, including 9 majors. Sorenstam had an amazing year in 2005. She earned her eighth Rolex Player of the Year award—the most in LPGA history. She also became the first player to sweep Rolex Player of the Year honors, the Vare Trophy, and the ADT Official Money List title five times. Sorenstam also earned her fifth consecutive Mizuno Classic title, making her the first golfer in LPGA history to win the same event five consecutive years.

10

The LPGA's
HIGHEST-PAID GOLFERS

Career winnings,
in millions of US dollars

Annika Sorenstam	Karrie Webb	Juli Inkster	Meg Mallon	Beth Daniel
$18.6 M	$11.0 M	$10.3 M	$8.8 M	$8.5 M

Man with the
Most Major Tournament Wins

Jack Nicklaus

Golfing great Jack Nicklaus has won a total of 18 major championships. His wins include 6 Masters, 5 PGAs, 4 U.S. Opens, and 3 British Opens. Nicklaus was named PGA Player of the Year five times. He was a member of the winning U.S. Ryder Cup team six times and was an individual World Cup winner a record three times. He was inducted into the World Golf Hall of Fame in 1974, just 12 years after he turned professional. He joined the U.S. Senior PGA Tour in 1990. In addition to playing the game, Nicklaus has designed close to 200 golf courses and written a number of popular books about the sport.

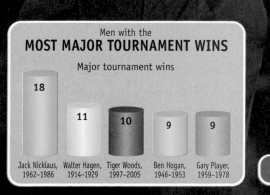

Men with the
MOST MAJOR TOURNAMENT WINS

Major tournament wins

Jack Nicklaus, 1962–1986	Walter Hagen, 1914–1929	Tiger Woods, 1997–2005	Ben Hogan, 1946–1953	Gary Player, 1959–1978
18	11	10	9	9

Women's Basketball Team with the Most NCAA Championships

Tennessee

The Tennessee Lady Volunteers have won six NCAA basketball championships. The Lady Vols won their latest championship in 1998, when they had a perfect record of 39–0, which was the most seasonal wins ever in women's collegiate basketball. In 2004, Tennessee was in the championship but was beaten by the University of Connecticut Huskies. Since 1976, an impressive 14 Lady Vols have been to the Olympics. And five Lady Vols have been inducted into the Women's Basketball Hall of Fame in Knoxville, Tennessee.

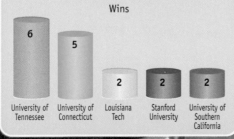

Women's Basketball Teams with the
MOST NCAA CHAMPIONSHIPS

Wins

Team	Wins
University of Tennessee	6
University of Connecticut	5
Louisiana Tech	2
Stanford University	2
University of Southern California	2

Men's Basketball Team with the
Most NCAA Championships

With 11 titles, the University of California, Los Angeles (UCLA) has the most NCAA Basketball Championship wins. The Bruins won their 11th championship in 1995. The school has won 23 of their last 41 league titles and has been in the NCAA playoffs for 35 of the last 41 years. During the final round of the NCAA championship in 2006, UCLA lost to the Florida Gators with a score of 73 to 57. Not surprisingly, UCLA has produced some basketball legends, too, including Kareem Abdul-Jabbar, Reggie Miller, and Baron Davis. For the last 36 years, the Bruins have called Pauley Pavilion home.

Men's Basketball Teams with the
MOST NCAA CHAMPIONSHIPS
Wins

UCLA	Kentucky	Indiana	North Carolina	Duke
11	7	5	4	3

NBA Team with the
Most Championship Titles

Boston Celtics

The Boston Celtics are the most successful team in the NBA with 16 championship wins. The first win came in 1957, and the team went on to win the next seven consecutive titles— the longest streak of consecutive championship wins in the history of U.S. sports. The most recent championship title came in 1986. The Celtics entered the Basketball Association of America in 1946, which later merged into the NBA in 1949. The Celtics have made the NBA playoffs for three consecutive seasons from 2001 to 2004, but they were eliminated in the first round each time.

NBA Teams with the
MOST CHAMPIONSHIP TITLES

Number of championship titles

Boston Celtics	Los Angeles Lakers	Chicago Bulls	Detroit Pistons	San Antonio Spurs
16	14	6	3	3

Highest Career
Scoring Average

Wilt Chamberlain and Michael Jordan

Both Michael Jordan and Wilt Chamberlain averaged an amazing 30.1 points per game during their legendary careers. Jordan played for the Chicago Bulls and the Washington Wizards. He led the league in scoring for seven years. During the 1986 season, he became only the second person ever to score 3,000 points. Chamberlain played for the Philadelphia Warriors, the Philadelphia 76ers, and the Los Angeles Lakers. In addition to the highest scoring average, he also holds the record for the most games with 50 or more points, with 118.

Players with the
HIGHEST CAREER SCORING AVERAGES

Average points per game

30.1	30.1	28.0	27.4	27.0
Wilt Chamberlain, 1959–1973	Michael Jordan, 1984–1998; 2001–2003	Allen Iverson, 1996–	Elgin Baylor, 1958–1971	Jerry West, 1960–1974

Michael Jordan

The NBA's
Highest-Scoring Team

Detroit Pistons

On December 13, 1983, the Detroit Pistons beat the Denver Nuggets with a score of 186 to 184 at McNichols Arena in Denver, Colorado. The game was tied at 145 at the end of regular play, and three overtime periods were needed to determine the winner. During the game, both the Pistons and the Nuggets each had six players who scored in the double figures. Four players scored more than 40 points each, which was an NBA first. The Pistons scored 74 field goals that night, claiming another NBA record that still stands today.

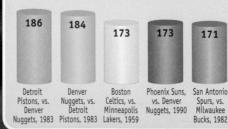

The NBA's
HIGHEST-SCORING TEAMS

Points scored by a team in one game

186	184	173	173	171
Detroit Pistons, vs. Denver Nuggets, 1983	Denver Nuggets, vs. Detroit Pistons, 1983	Boston Celtics, vs. Minneapolis Lakers, 1959	Phoenix Suns, vs. Denver Nuggets, 1990	San Antonio Spurs, vs. Milwaukee Bucks, 1982

NBA Player with the
Highest Salary

Shaquille O'Neal

Shaquille O'Neal earned a record $33.4 million as the starting center for the Miami Heat in 2005. O'Neal began his professional career with the Orlando Magic in 1992 as the first overall draft pick, and was later named NBA Rookie of the Year. He was the regular season scoring champion in 1995 and 2000, and played in the All-Star Game nine times between 1993 and 2002. O'Neal also led the league in field goal percentage five times between 1993 and 2001. In addition to the NBA, O'Neal took home a gold medal as part of the U.S. Olympic team in 1996.

NBA Players with the
HIGHEST SALARIES

Annual salaries,
in millions of US dollars

| $20.0 M | $19.1 M | $19.1 M | $18.6 M | $18.0 M |
| Shaquille O'Neal | Allan Houston | Chris Webber | Michael Finley | Kevin Garnett |

WNBA Player with the Highest
Free Throw Scoring Average

Eva Nemcova

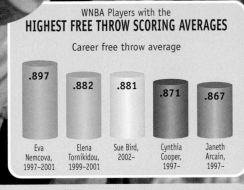

WNBA Players with the
HIGHEST FREE THROW SCORING AVERAGES

Career free throw average

.897	.882	.881	.871	.867
Eva Nemcova, 1997–2001	Elena Tornikidou, 1999–2001	Sue Bird, 2002–	Cynthia Cooper, 1997–	Janeth Arcain, 1997–

With a free throw average of .897, Eva Nemcova was not a person to foul. The six-foot-three-inch- (1.9 m) tall guard played for the Cleveland Rockers from 1997 to 2001. She was the fourth overall draft pick in the league's inaugural year and was named to the WNBA First Team that season. In 1999, Nemcova became the ninth person in the WNBA to score more than 1,000 points. In 2000, she set a WNBA free throw record when she made 66 consecutive shots that season. Nemcova retired in 2001 after an ACL injury.

Most Career
Points

Kareem Abdul-Jabbar

During his highly successful career, Kareem Abdul-Jabbar scored a total of 38,387 points. In 1969, Abdul-Jabbar began his NBA tenure with the Milwaukee Bucks. He was named Rookie of the Year in 1970. The following year he scored 2,596 points and helped the Bucks win the NBA championship. He was traded to the Los Angeles Lakers in 1975. With his new team, Abdul-Jabbar won the NBA championship in 1980, 1982, 1985, 1987, and 1988. He retired from basketball in 1989 and was inducted into the Basketball Hall of Fame in 1995.

Players with the
MOST CAREER POINTS

Points scored

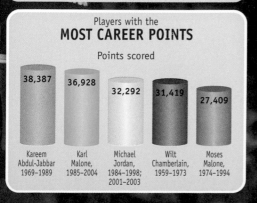

38,387	36,928	32,292	31,419	27,409
Kareem Abdul-Jabbar 1969–1989	Karl Malone, 1985–2004	Michael Jordan, 1984–1998; 2001–2003	Wilt Chamberlain, 1959–1973	Moses Malone, 1974–1994

WNBA Player with the
Highest Career PPG Average

Cynthia Cooper

Houston Comets guard Cynthia Cooper played in the WNBA from 1997 to 2000 and averaged 21.0 points per game (PPG). She later returned to the Comets in 2003 and played four games that season before retiring. Cooper was a three-time WNBA scoring champion in 1997, 1998, and 1999, and she was the first player in the league to reach the 500, 1,000, 2,000, and 2,500 point marks.

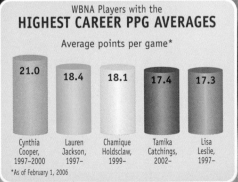

WBNA Players with the
HIGHEST CAREER PPG AVERAGES
Average points per game*

21.0	18.4	18.1	17.4	17.3
Cynthia Cooper, 1997–2000	Lauren Jackson, 1997–	Chamique Holdsclaw, 1999–	Tamika Catchings, 2002–	Lisa Leslie, 1997–

*As of February 1, 2006

WNBA Player with the
Most Career Points

Lisa Leslie

Lisa Leslie—center for the Los Angeles Sparks—has scored 4,732 points in her career. Leslie has a career average of 17.3 points per game. She was named MVP of the WNBA All-Star Games in 1999, 2001, and 2002. Leslie was also a member of the 1996 and 2000 Olympic gold-medal-winning women's basketball teams. In both 2001 and 2002, Leslie led her team to victory in the WNBA championship and was named Finals MVP. Leslie set another record on July 30, 2002, when she became the first player in WNBA history to slam dunk in a game.

WNBA Players with the
MOST CAREER POINTS

Points scored*

4,732	3,894	3,851	3,729	3,521
Lisa Leslie, 1997–	Sheryl Swoopes, 1997–	Tina Thompson, 1997–	Katie Smith, 2000–	Chamique Holdsclaw, 1999–

*As of May 2, 2006

Highest Seasonal
Home Run Total

Barry Bonds

Baseball's Top Seasonal
HOME RUN HITTERS
Number of home runs

73	70	66	65	64
Barry Bonds, 2001	Mark McGwire, 1998	Sammy Sosa, 1998	Mark McGwire, 1999	Sammy Sosa, 2001

On October 5, 2001, Barry Bonds smashed Mark McGwire's record for seasonal home runs when he hit his 71st home run in the first inning of a game against the Los Angeles Dodgers. Two innings later, he hit number 72. Bonds, a left fielder for the San Francisco Giants, has a career total of 708 home runs. He also holds the records for seasonal walks (198) and seasonal on-base percentage (0.582). Bonds and his father, hitting coach Bobby Bonds, hold the all-time father-son home run record with 994.

World's All-Time Home Run Hitter

Hank Aaron

In 1974, Hank Aaron broke Babe Ruth's lifetime record of 714 home runs. By the time he retired from baseball in 1976, Aaron had hit a total of 755 homers—a record that has remained unbroken. His amazing hitting ability earned him the nickname "Hammerin' Hank." Aaron holds many other distinguished baseball records, including most lifetime runs batted in (2,297) and most years with 30 or more home runs (15). Aaron was an excellent defensive player, earning three Gold Glove Awards.

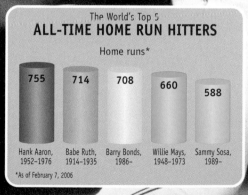

The World's Top 5
ALL-TIME HOME RUN HITTERS

Home runs*

755	714	708	660	588
Hank Aaron, 1952–1976	Babe Ruth, 1914–1935	Barry Bonds, 1986–	Willie Mays, 1948–1973	Sammy Sosa, 1989–

*As of February 7, 2006

Most
Career Strikeouts

Nolan Ryan

Nolan Ryan leads Major League Baseball with an incredible 5,714 career strikeouts. In his impressive 28-year career, he played for the New York Mets, the California Angels, the Houston Astros, and the Texas Rangers. The right-handed pitcher from Refugio, Texas, led the American League in strikeouts 10 times. In 1989, at the age of 42, Ryan became the oldest pitcher ever to lead the Major League in strikeouts. Ryan set another record in 1991 when he pitched his seventh career no-hitter.

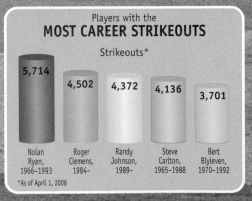

Players with the
MOST CAREER STRIKEOUTS

Strikeouts*

5,714	4,502	4,372	4,136	3,701
Nolan Ryan, 1966–1993	Roger Clemens, 1984–	Randy Johnson, 1989–	Steve Carlton, 1965–1988	Bert Blyleven, 1970–1992

*As of April 1, 2006

Most
Career Hits

Pete Rose

Rose belted an amazing 4,256 hits during his 23 years of professional baseball. He got his record-setting hit in 1985, when he was a player-manager for the Cincinnati Reds. By the time Pete Rose retired as a player from Major League Baseball in 1986, he had set several other career records. Rose holds the Major League records for the most career games (3,562), the most times at bat (14,053), and the most seasons with more than 200 hits (10). During his career, he played for the Cincinnati Reds, the Philadelphia Phillies, and the Montreal Expos.

Players with the
MOST CAREER HITS

Hits

Pete Rose, 1963–1986	Ty Cobb, 1905–1928	Hank Aaron, 1952–1976	Stan Musial, 1941–1963	Tris Speaker, 1907–1928
4,256	4,191	3,771	3,630	3,514

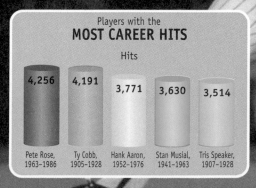

Baseball Player with the Most
Expensive Contract

Alex Rodriguez

Alex Rodriguez signed a 10-year deal with the Texas Rangers for $252 million in 2001. This does not include any bonuses the shortstop may earn for winning titles or awards, or any money he could make from potential endorsements. The right-hander began his successful career with Seattle in 1994. In 2004, Rodriguez joined the New York Yankees, and the ball club is now responsible for paying the majority of his contract. In 2005, Rodriguez won the American League MVP award.

Baseball Players with the
MOST EXPENSIVE CONTRACTS

Yearly salary, in
millions of US dollars

$21.7 M	$20.6 M	$19.3 M	$18.3 M	$18.0 M
Alex Rodriguez, New York Yankees	Derek Jeter, New York Yankees	Barry Bonds, San Francisco Giants	Manny Ramirez, Boston Red Sox	Roger Clemens, Houston Astros

MLB Player with the
Most Career Runs

Rickey Henderson

During his 25 years in the majors, baseball great Rickey Henderson boasts the most career runs with 2,295. Henderson got his start with the Oakland Athletics in 1979, and went on to play for the Yankees, the Mets, the Mariners, the Red Sox, the Padres, the Dodgers, and the Angels. Henderson won a Gold Glove Award in 1981, and the American League MVP award in 1989 and 1990. Henderson is also known as the "Man of Steal" because he holds the MLB record for most stolen bases in a career with 1,406.

MLB Players with the
MOST CAREER RUNS

Career runs

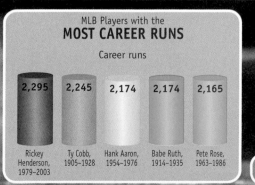

2,295	2,245	2,174	2,174	2,165
Rickey Henderson, 1979–2003	Ty Cobb, 1905–1928	Hank Aaron, 1954–1976	Babe Ruth, 1914–1935	Pete Rose, 1963–1986

27

Most MVP Awards in the American League

Yogi Berra, Joe DiMaggio, Jimmie Foxx, and Mickey Mantle

With three honors each, Yogi Berra, Joe DiMaggio, Jimmie Foxx, and Mickey Mantle all hold the record for the Most Valuable Player awards during their professional careers. DiMaggio, Berra, and Mantle were all New York Yankees. Foxx played for the Athletics, the Cubs, and the Phillies. The player with the biggest gap between wins was DiMaggio, who won his first award in 1939 and his last in 1947. Also nicknamed "Joltin' Joe" and the "Yankee Clipper," DiMaggio began playing in the major leagues in 1936. The following year, he led the league in home runs and runs scored. He was elected to the Baseball Hall of Fame in 1955.

Joe DiMaggio

Players with the
MOST AMERICAN LEAGUE MVP AWARDS

Most Valuable Player (MVP) awards

Yogi Berra, 1946–1963; 1965	Joe DiMaggio, 1936–1951	Jimmie Foxx, 1925–1945	Mickey Mantle, 1951–1960	Alex Rodriguez, 1994–
3	3	3	3	2

Most MVP Awards in the
National League

San Francisco Giant Barry Bonds has earned seven Most Valuable Player awards for his amazing achievements in the National Baseball League. He received his first two MVP awards in 1990 and 1992 while playing for the Pittsburgh Pirates. The next five awards came while wearing the Giants uniform in 1993, 2001, 2002, 2003, and 2004. Bonds is the first player to win an MVP award three times in consecutive seasons. In fact, Bonds is the only baseball player in history to have won more than three MVP awards.

Barry Bonds

Players with the
MOST NATIONAL LEAGUE MVP AWARDS

Most Valuable Player (MVP) awards

7	3	3	3	2
Barry Bonds, 1986–	Roy Campanella, 1948–1957	Stan Musial, 1941–1963	Mike Schmidt, 1972–1989	Ernie Banks, 1953–1971

29

Team with the
Most World Series Wins

New York Yankees

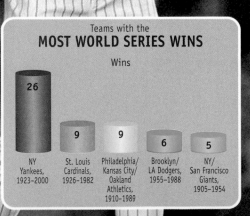

Between 1923 and 2000, the New York Yankees were the World Series champions a record 26 times. The team picked up their latest win in October of 2000 when they beat the New York Mets. The Yankees beat the Mets four games to one to win their third consecutive championship. Since their early days, the team has included some of baseball's greatest players, including Babe Ruth, Lou Gehrig, Yogi Berra, Joe DiMaggio, and Mickey Mantle.

Teams with the
MOST WORLD SERIES WINS

Wins

26	9	9	6	5
NY Yankees, 1923–2000	St. Louis Cardinals, 1926–1982	Philadelphia/ Kansas City/ Oakland Athletics, 1910–1989	Brooklyn/ LA Dodgers, 1955–1988	NY/ San Francisco Giants, 1905–1954

Most
Cy Young Awards

Roger Clemens, a starting pitcher for the Houston Astros, has earned a record seven Cy Young awards during his career so far. He set a Major League record in April 1986 when he struck out 20 batters in one game. He later tied this record in September 1996. In September 2001, Clemens became the first Major League pitcher to win 20 of his first 21 decisions in one season. In June 2003, he became the first pitcher in more than a decade to win his 300th game. He also struck out his 4,000th batter that year.

Roger Clemens

Pitchers with the
MOST CY YOUNG AWARDS

Cy Young awards

7	5	4	4	3
Roger Clemens, 1984–	Randy Johnson, 1988–	Steve Carlton, 1965–1988	Greg Maddux, 1986–	Sandy Koufax, 1955–1966

Player with the Most At Bats

Pete Rose

Pete Rose has stood behind the plate for 14,053 at bats—more than any other Major League player. Rose signed with the Cincinnati Reds after graduating high school in 1963 and played second base. During his impressive career, Rose set several other records, including the most singles in the Major Leagues (3,315), most seasons with 600 or more at bats in the major leagues (17), most career doubles in the National League (746), and most career runs in the National League (2,165). He was also named World Series MVP, *Sports Illustrated* Sportsman of the Year, and *The Sporting News* Man of the Year.

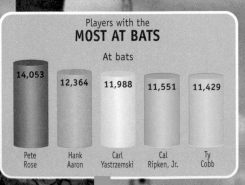

Players with the MOST AT BATS

At bats

Pete Rose	Hank Aaron	Carl Yastrzemski	Cal Ripken, Jr.	Ty Cobb
14,053	12,364	11,988	11,551	11,429

Player with the
Most Career RBIs

Hank Aaron

During his 23 years in the major leagues, right-handed Hank Aaron batted in an incredible 2,297 runs. Aaron began his professional career with the Indianapolis Clowns, a team in the Negro American League, in 1952. He was traded to the Milwaukee Braves in 1954 and won the National League batting championship with an average of .328. He was named the league's Most Valuable Player a year later when he led his team to a World Series victory. Aaron retired as a player in 1976 and was inducted into the Baseball Hall of Fame in 1982.

Players with the
MOST CAREER RBIs
Runs batted in

2,297	2,213	2,076	1,995	1,951
Hank Aaron, 1952–1976	Babe Ruth, 1914–1935	Cap Anson, 1876–1897	Lou Gehrig, 1923–1939	Stan Musial, 1941–1963

Player Who Played the
Most Consecutive Games

Cal Ripken, Jr.

Players with the
MOST CONSECUTIVE GAMES PLAYED

Consecutive games played

2,632	2,130	1,307	1,207	1,117
Cal Ripken, Jr., 1978–2001	Lou Gehrig, 1923–1939	Everett Scott, 1914–1925	Steve Garvey, 1968–1988	Billy Williams, 1959–1974

Baltimore Oriole Cal Ripken, Jr., played 2,632 consecutive games from May 30, 1982, to September 20, 1998. The right-handed third baseman also holds the record for the most consecutive innings played: 8,243. In June 1996, Ripken also broke the world record for consecutive games with 2,216, surpassing Sachio Kinugasa of Japan. When he played as a shortstop, Ripken set Major League records for most home runs (345) and most extra base hits (855) for his position. He has started in the All-Star Game a record 19 times in a row.

Quarterback with the
Most Passing Yards

Dan Marino

Dan Marino has racked up 61,361 passing yards during his 17-year career. Marino was selected by the Dolphins as the twenty-seventh pick in the first-round draft in 1983. He remained a Dolphin for the rest of his career, setting many impressive records. Marino has the most career pass attempts (8,358), the most career completions (4,967), the most career touchdown passes (420), the most passing yards in a season (5,084), and the most seasons leading the league in completions (6). Marino retired from the NFL in 2000.

Players with the
MOST PASSING YARDS

Yards

61,361	53,615	51,475	49,325	47,003
Dan Marino, 1983–2000	Brett Favre, 1991–	John Elway, 1983–1999	Warren Moon, 1984–2000	Fran Tarkenton, 1961–1978

Highest Career
Rushing Total

Emmitt Smith

Running back Emmitt Smith holds the record for all-time rushing yards with 18,355. Smith began his career with the Dallas Cowboys in 1990 and played with the team until the end of the 2002 season. In 2003, Smith signed a two-year contract with the Arizona Cardinals. Smith also holds the NFL records for the most carries with 4,142 and the most rushing touchdowns with 164.

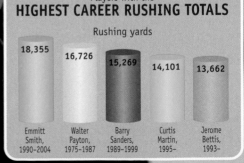

Players with the
HIGHEST CAREER RUSHING TOTALS

Rushing yards

18,355	16,726	15,269	14,101	13,662
Emmitt Smith, 1990–2004	Walter Payton, 1975–1987	Barry Sanders, 1989–1999	Curtis Martin, 1995–	Jerome Bettis, 1993–

Most Career
Touchdowns

Jerry Rice

Jerry Rice has scored a record 207 touchdowns. He is widely considered to be one of the greatest wide receivers ever to play in the National Football League. Rice holds a total of 14 NFL records, including career receptions (1,549), receiving yards (22,895), receiving touchdowns (197), consecutive 100-catch seasons (4), most games with 100 receiving yards (73), and many others. He was named NFL Player of the Year twice, *Sports Illustrated* Player of the Year four times, and NFL Offensive Player of the Year once. Rice retired from the NFL in 2005.

Players with the
MOST CAREER TOUCHDOWNS
Touchdowns scored

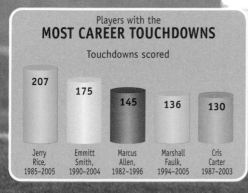

Jerry Rice, 1985–2005	Emmitt Smith, 1990–2004	Marcus Allen, 1982–1996	Marshall Faulk, 1994–2005	Cris Carter 1987–2003
207	175	145	136	130

Most Single-Season Touchdowns

Shaun Alexander

Players with the
MOST SINGLE-SEASON TOUCHDOWNS
Touchdowns scored

28	27	26	25	24
Shaun Alexander, 2005	Priest Holmes, 2003	Marshall Faulk, 2000	Emmitt Smith, 1995	John Riggins, 1983

Seattle Seahawks running back Shaun Alexander scored 28 touchdowns in the 2005 season. He had 27 rushing touchdowns and one receiving touchdown, and became the first player in NFL history to score 15 or more touchdowns in five consecutive seasons. He also led the league in rushing that year with 1,880 yards. For all of these achievements, Alexander was named league MVP in 2005.

During his six-year NFL career, Alexander has scored a total of 100 touchdowns and rushed for 7,817 yards.

Highest Career Scoring Total

Gary Anderson

Gary Anderson has scored 2,434 points in his 23 seasons of professional play. In 1998, the NFL's top kicker hit 35-of-35 field goals and became the first NFL player to go an entire season without missing a kick. Anderson began his career with the Pittsburgh Steelers in 1982 and later played with the Philadelphia Eagles and the San Francisco 49ers. He joined the Vikings in 1998 and scored 542 points for them— the fifth-highest in team history. Anderson joined the Tennessee Titans in 2003 and played for two seasons before retiring.

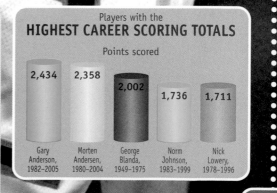

Players with the
HIGHEST CAREER SCORING TOTALS

Points scored

Gary Anderson, 1982–2005	Morten Andersen, 1980–2004	George Blanda, 1949–1975	Norm Johnson, 1983–1999	Nick Lowery, 1978–1996
2,434	2,358	2,002	1,736	1,711

Team with the Most
Super Bowl Wins

Cowboys, 49ers, and Steelers

With five championships each, the Dallas Cowboys, the San Francisco 49ers, and the Pittsburgh Steelers all hold the record for the most Super Bowl wins. The first championship win for the Cowboys was in 1972, which was followed by wins in 1978, 1993, 1994, and 1996. Out of those 10 victories, the game with the most spectators was Super Bowl XXVII, when Dallas defeated the Buffalo Bills at the Rose Bowl in Pasadena, California, in 1993. The 49ers had their first win in 1982, and repeated their victory in 1985, 1989, 1990, and 1995.

Teams with the
MOST SUPER BOWL WINS

Super Bowls won

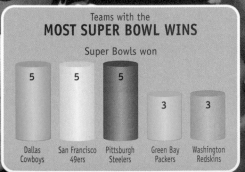

Dallas Cowboys	San Francisco 49ers	Pittsburgh Steelers	Green Bay Packers	Washington Redskins
5	5	5	3	3

Top-Winning NFL Coach

Don Shula

Top-Winning
NFL COACHES

Games won

347	324	270	229	167
Don Shula, 1963–1995	George Halas, 1922–1929, 1933–1941, 1946–1955, 1958–1967	Tom Landry, 1960–1988	Curly Lambeau, 1919–1957	Paul Brown, 1946–1962

Don Shula led his teams to a remarkable 347 wins during his 33 years as a head coach in the National Football League. When Shula became head coach of the Baltimore Colts in 1963, he became the youngest head coach in football history. He stayed with the team until 1969 and reached the playoffs four times. Shula became the head coach for the Miami Dolphins in 1970 and coached them until 1995. During this time, the Dolphins reached the playoffs 20 times and won at least 10 games a season 21 times. After leading them to Super Bowl wins in 1972 and 1973, Shula became one of only five coaches to win the championship in back-to-back years.

The NFL's
Highest-Paid Player

Michael Vick

Michael Vick earned an unprecedented $37.5 million in 2005 as the starting quarterback for the Atlanta Falcons. Vick joined the Falcons in 2001 from Virginia Tech as the top overall draft pick that year. During the past five seasons, Vick has totaled more than 9,000 passing yards, and has run the ball into the end zone himself an amazing 70 times. He played in the 2002 and 2005 Pro Bowls. In 2004, he became the first quarterback to ever throw for more than 250 yards and rush for more than 100 yards in the same game. Vick has a career quarterback rating of 75.8.

The NFL's
HIGHEST-PAID FOOTBALL PLAYERS

Annual salary, in millions of US dollars

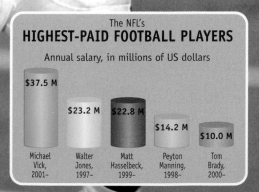

$37.5 M	$23.2 M	$22.8 M	$14.2 M	$10.0 M
Michael Vick, 2001–	Walter Jones, 1997–	Matt Hasselbeck, 1999–	Peyton Manning, 1998–	Tom Brady, 2000–

NFL Team with the
Most Consecutive Games Won

New England Patriots

NFL Teams with the
MOST CONSECUTIVE GAMES WON

Consecutive games won

18	17	16	16	16
New England Patriots, 2003–2004	Chicago Bears, 1933–1934	Chicago Bears, 1941–1942	Miami Dolphins, 1971–1973	Miami Dolphins, 1983–1984

The New England Patriots won 18 consecutive games during the 2003 and 2004 seasons. After finishing September 2003 with 2 wins and 2 losses, the team went on to win the next 15 games, including Super Bowl XXXVIII. When the 2004 season began, the team continued its winning streak for the next six games. The Patriots finished the season 14-2, and went on to win Super Bowl XXXIX. With this win, the Patriots became the second team in NFL history to win three championships in four years.

World's Top-Earning
Female Tennis Player

Steffi Graf

Steffi Graf earned $21.8 million during her 17-year career. After turning professional at age 13, Graf scored 902 victories, including 22 Grand Slam singles titles and 107 tournament titles. During her career, she was ranked number one for 377 weeks and named the WTA Player of the Year seven times. Graf's most successful year in tennis came in 1988 when she won 96% of her matches, all four Grand Slam singles titles, and an Olympic gold medal. Graf retired in 1999 and is married to tennis superstar Andre Agassi.

The World's Top-Earning
FEMALE TENNIS PLAYERS

Career earnings,
in millions of US dollars

$21.8 M	$21.5 M	$21.2 M	$18.8 M	$16.9 M
Steffi Graf, 1982–1999	Lindsey Davenport, 1993–	Martina Navratilova, 1975–1994	Martina Hingis, 1994–2003	Arantxa Sanchez-Vicario, 1988–2002

World's Top-Earning
Male Tennis Player

Pete Sampras

Pete Sampras has earned more than $43 million during his 13 years as a professional tennis player. That averages out to about $9,060 a day! In addition to being the top-earning male tennis player of all time, Sampras also holds several other titles. He has been named ATP Player of the Year a record six times, he has the most career game wins with 762, and he has been ranked number one for the most weeks with 276. Sampras also ranks fourth in all-time career singles titles with 64. Sampras retired from tennis in 2003, but returned to the game in 2006 when he signed on to play for the World Team Tennis Pro League.

The World's Top-Earning
MALE TENNIS PLAYERS

Career earnings,
in millions of US dollars

Player	Earnings
Pete Sampras, 1990–2003	$43.3 M
Andre Agassi, 1986–	$30.8 M
Boris Becker, 1984–1997	$25.1 M
Yevgeny Kafelnikov, 1992–2004	$23.9 M
Roger Federer, 1998–	$22.6 M

Woman with the
Most Singles Grand Slam Titles

Women with the
MOST SINGLES GRAND SLAM TITLES

Titles won

24	22	19	18	18
Margaret Court Smith, 1960–1975	Steffi Graff, 1987–1999	Helen Wills-Moody, 1923–1938	Chris Evert-Lloyd, 1974–1986	Martina Navratilova, 1974–1995

Margaret Court Smith won 24 Grand Slam singles titles between 1960 and 1975. She is the only woman ever to win the French, British, U.S., and Australian titles during one year in both the singles and doubles competitions. She was only the second woman to win all four titles in the same year. During her amazing career, she won a total of 66 Grand Slam championships—more than any other woman. Court was the world's top-seeded female player from 1962 to 1965, 1969 to 1970, and 1973. She was inducted into the International Tennis Hall of Fame in 1979.

Margaret Court Smith

Man with the Most Singles
Grand Slam Titles

Pete Sampras

Men with the
MOST SINGLES GRAND SLAM TITLES

Titles won

14	12	11	11	10
Pete Sampras, 1990–2002	Roy Emerson, 1961–1967	Bjorn Borg, 1974–1981	Rod Laver, 1960–1969	Bill Tilden, 1920–1930

With 14 victories, Pete Sampras holds the title for the most Grand Slam male singles titles. He has won two Australian Opens, seven Wimbledon titles, and five U.S. Opens between 1990 and 2002. After not winning a major title in two years, Sampras won a surprise victory at the 2002 U.S. Open. He was the number 17 seed and beat Andre Agassi in a three-hour final match. After a three-year retirement, Sampras began playing for the World Tennis Team in 2006.

Top Female World-Champion Figure Skaters

Carol Heiss/ Michelle Kwan

Carol Heiss and Michelle Kwan—two of America's most successful figure skaters—have each won the Women's World Figure Skating Championships five times. Heiss, whose wins came between 1956 and 1960, also won an Olympic silver medal for women's figure skating in 1956, and then a gold medal during the 1960 Winter Olympics in Squaw Valley, California. Kwan won the World Championships in 1996, 1998, 2000, 2001, and 2003. Kwan has also won the Women's U.S. Championships a record six times. She picked up a silver medal in the 1998 Olympics and won a bronze in 2002. Kwan went to compete in the 2006 Winter Games, but she had to pull out of the competition when—after qualifying—a groin injury prevented her from continuing.

Michelle Kwan

Women with the
MOST WORLD FIGURE-SKATING CHAMPIONSHIP WINS

World Championship wins

Carol Heiss, USA, 1956–1960	Michelle Kwan, USA, 1996–2003	Katarina Witt, E. Germany, 1984–1988	Sjoukje Dijkstra, Netherlands, 1962–1964	Peggy Fleming, USA, 1966–1968
5	5	4	3	3

Top Male World-Champion
Figure Skaters

Kurt Browning, Scott Hamilton, Hayes Jenkins, and Alexei Yagudin

Alexei Yagudin

Figure skaters Kurt Browning, Scott Hamilton, Hayes Jenkins, and Alexei Yagudin have each won four world championship competitions. Yagudin is from Russia and won his World Championship titles in 1998, 2000, 2001, and 2002. In the 2001–2002 season, Yagudin became the first male skater to win a gold medal in the four major skating events—Europeans, Grand Prix Final, Worlds, and the Olympics—in the same year. Yagudin retired in 2003 due to a hip disorder. Browning is from Canada and was inducted into the Canadian Sports Hall of Fame in 1994. Hamilton and Jenkins are from the United States. Hamilton won the competitions from 1981 to 1984. He also won a gold medal in the 1984 Olympics. Jenkins's impressive skating career included winning every major championship between 1953 and 1956.

Men with the
MOST WORLD FIGURE-SKATING CHAMPIONSHIP WINS

World Championship wins

Kurt Browning, Canada, 1989–1993	Scott Hamilton, USA, 1981–1984	Hayes Jenkins, USA, 1953–1956	Alexei Yagudin, Russia, 1988–2002	Yevgeny Plushchenko, Russia, 2001–2004
4	4	4	4	3

Fastest Woman in the Olympic
100 Meters

Florence Griffith-Joyner

At the 1988 Seoul Olympic Games, Florence Griffith-Joyner—also known as Flo Jo—sprinted the 100 meters (328 ft) in just 10.54 seconds. She won two more gold medals for the 200-meter (656-ft) dash and the 100-meter (328-ft) relay that year. Flo Jo also added a silver medal at the Games in the 400-meter (1,312-ft) relay. Flo Jo holds the world records for both the 100- and 200-meter dashes, and is one of only two women to ever run the 200 meters (656 ft) in under 21.70 seconds. For all of her impressive achievements, she was named the Associated Press Athlete of the Year, and the U.S. Olympic Committee Sportswoman of the Year in 1988. Flo Jo passed away in 1998.

Fastest Woman in the Olympic
100 METERS
Time in seconds

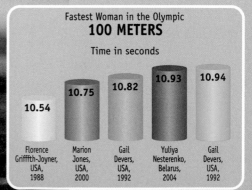

Florence Grifffth-Joyner, USA, 1988	Marion Jones, USA, 2000	Gail Devers, USA, 1992	Yuliya Nesterenko, Belarus, 2004	Gail Devers, USA, 1992
10.54	10.75	10.82	10.93	10.94

Fastest Man in the Olympic
100 Meters

Donovan Bailey

At the 1996 Atlanta Games, Canadian sprinter Donovan Bailey set an Olympic record when he completed the 100 meters (328 ft) in 9.84 seconds. That means Donovan was running at a speed of about 22.7 miles (36.5 km) per hour. He also took home a gold medal in the 4 X 100 meter event. Donovan became the first of only two men ever to hold all three titles of Olympic Champion, World Champion, and World Record Holder at the same time. Bailey retired from competitive racing in 2001, and the five-time World and Olympic Champion donates a lot of his time to charity.

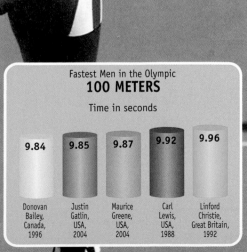

Fastest Men in the Olympic
100 METERS

Time in seconds

9.84	9.85	9.87	9.92	9.96
Donovan Bailey, Canada, 1996	Justin Gatlin, USA, 2004	Maurice Greene, USA, 2004	Carl Lewis, USA, 1988	Linford Christie, Great Britain, 1992

51

Fastest
Men's 100m Freestyle Swim

Pieter van den Hoogenband

At the 2004 Summer Olympics in Athens, Greece, Pieter van den Hoogenband broke his own Olympic record with a time of 48.17 seconds in the 100-meter (328-ft) freestyle swimming event. Van den Hoogenband, a native of the Netherlands, also won two silver medals in Athens—one for the 200-meter (656-ft) freestyle and one for the 100-meter (328-ft) relay. This speedy swimmer was also very successful in the 2000 Olympics in Sydney, Australia, winning two gold medals and two bronze.

Fastest
MEN'S 100M FREESTYLE SWIM

Time in seconds

48.17	Pieter van den Hoogenband, Netherlands, 2004
48.30	Pieter van den Hoogenband, Netherlands, 2000
48.63	Matt Biondi, USA, 1988
48.74	Aleksandr Popov, Russia, 1996
49.02	Aleksandr Popov, Unifed Team, 1992

Fastest
Women's 100m Freestyle Swim

Dutch swimmer Inge de Bruijn took home the gold in the women's 100-meter (328-ft) freestyle swim at the 2000 Olympic Games in Sydney, Australia, with a time of 53.83 seconds. De Bruijn also won gold medals in the 50-meter (164-ft) freestyle and the 100-meter (328-ft) butterfly that year, setting world records in all three medal-winning events. In addition, she picked up a silver medal in the 100-meter (328-ft) freestyle relay. De Bruijn's success continued at the 2004 Games in Athens, where she won a gold in the 50-meter (164-ft) freestyle, a silver in the 100-meter (328-ft) freestyle, and two bronze for the 100-meter (328-ft) butterfly and 100-meter (328-ft) relay.

Inge de Bruijn

Fastest
WOMEN'S 100M FREESTYLE SWIM

Time in seconds

53.83	53.84	54.50	54.64	54.79
Inge de Bruijn, Netherlands, 2000	Jodie Henry, Australia, 2004	Li Jingyi, China, 1996	Zhuang, Yong, China, 1992	Barbara Krause, E. Germany, 1980

Fastest Woman in Olympic Downhill Skiing

Michela Figini

At the 1984 Olympic Games in Sarajevo, Yugoslavia, skiing sensation Michela Figini of Switzerland won the downhill skiing gold medal, with a time of 1:13.36. At the age of 17, Figini became the youngest Olympian to earn a medal in Alpine skiing. She became known for her strict self-discipline during training and her graceful moves on the course. Figini is a native of southern Ticino, Switzerland, and speaks fluent Italian.

Fastest Women in Olympic
DOWNHILL SKIING

Time (minutes:seconds)

Michela Figini, Switzerland, 1984	Marina Kiehl, W. Germany, 1988	Katja Seizinger, Germany, 1998	Katja Seizinger, Germany, 1994	Marie-Thérèse Nadig, Switzerland, 1972
1:13.36	1:25.86	1:28.89	1:35.93	1:36.68

Fastest Man in Olympic
Downhill Skiing

Fritz Strobl

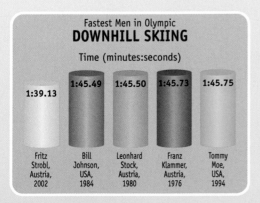

Fastest Men in Olympic
DOWNHILL SKIING

Time (minutes:seconds)

Fritz Strobl, Austria, 2002	Bill Johnson, USA, 1984	Leonhard Stock, Austria, 1980	Franz Klammer, Austria, 1976	Tommy Moe, USA, 1994
1:39.13	1:45.49	1:45.50	1:45.73	1:45.75

Austrian skier Fritz Strobl flew down the course and grabbed the gold with a time of 1:39.13 during the 2002 Olympics in Salt Lake City, Utah. At times, Strobl reached speeds of 80 miles (129 km) per hour. The 1.9-mile (3.1-km) course—nicknamed The Grizzly—was said to be one of the toughest in Olympic competition. It was shorter than most other courses, but it included a vertical drop of 3,000 feet (914 m) and wound through the Wasatch-Cache National Forest. Strobl, a 29-year-old policeman from Lienz, also won two other major competitions the same year—Bormio and Garmisch-Partenkirchen.

World's Fastest Olympic
Bobsled Time

Germany II

World's Fastest Olympic
BOBSLED TIMES

Time (minutes:seconds)

				3:40.42
			3:27.28	
		3:20.22		
	3:07.51			
2:39.41				
Germany II, 1998	Germany II, 2002	E. Germany, 1984	Germany, 1994	Germany, 2006

Germany II sped down the bobsled track and into the history books with a record-breaking time of 2:39.41 at the 1998 Winter Olympics in Nagano, Japan. That speedy time was 0.6 seconds faster than the second-place finish! The team of four men—Christoph Langen, Markus Zimmermann, Marco Jakobs, and Olaf Hampel—followed the German tradition of excellence in bobsledding. In fact, the five fastest bobsled times were all accomplished by Germans. A bobsled can reach a speed of 90 miles (145 km) per hour, and the crew feels five times the force of gravity when braking. The sport became an Olympic competition in 1924.

Athletes with the
Most Medals in One Olympics

Aleksandr Dityatin/ Michael Phelps

In separate Olympics, Aleksandr Dityatin and Michael Phelps each won a total of eight medals. Dityatin was a Soviet gymnast in the 1980 Olympics in Moscow, Soviet Union. Competing in front of the hometown crowd, he took gold in the team competition and the individual all-around. Dityatin then won six medals in one day: one gold, four silvers, and one bronze. In the 2004 Olympics in Athens, Greece, Phelps swam his way to six gold medals and two bronze. He was the first American male to qualify for six individual events. Phelps holds three Olympic records.

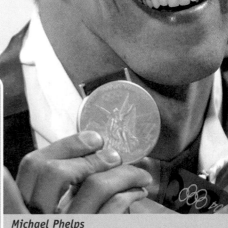

Michael Phelps

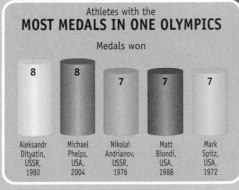

Athletes with the
MOST MEDALS IN ONE OLYMPICS

Medals won

Aleksandr Dityatin, USSR, 1980	Michael Phelps, USA, 2004	Nikolai Andrianov, USSR, 1976	Matt Biondi, USA, 1988	Mark Spitz, USA, 1972
8	8	7	7	7

Man with the
Most CAPS

Claudio Suárez

Mexican soccer star Claudio Suárez has the most CAPS, or international games played, with 172. Suárez had his international debut in July 1992 while playing for the UNAM Pumas. Since then he has also played for the Chivas de Guadalajara and the San Nicolas de los Garza Tigres. Nicknamed the Emperor, Suárez has scored 42 goals in competition. Suárez also played in the 1994 and 1998 World Cups. In 2006, he joined Chivas USA—a MLS expansion club based in the United States.

Men with the
MOST CAPS

Total international games played

Claudio Suárez, Mexico, 1992–	Mohamed Al-Deayea, Saudi Arabia, 1990–	Adnan Khamées Al-Talyani, UAE, 1984–1997	Cobi Jones, United States, 1992–	Hossam Hassan, Egypt, 1985–
172	170	164	164	163

Country with the Most
World Cup Points

Brazil

Countries with the
MOST WORLD CUP POINTS

Total points

Brazil, 1958–2002	Germany/ W. Germany, 1954–2002	Italy, 1934–1982	Argentina, 1978–1986	Uruguay, 1930–1950
30	29	21	14	10

Since winning their first championship in 1958, Brazil has accumulated 30 points in World Cup championships. (A win is worth four points, runner-up is worth three points, third place is worth two points, and fourth place is worth one point.) Their latest win came in 2002 when they defeated Germany with a score of 2-0. In Brazil, soccer is both the national sport and the national pastime. Many Brazilian superstar players are even considered national heroes. Some of Brazil's most recent stars include Ronaldo and Rivaldo—top scorers in the 2002 World Cup. The World Cup was organized by the Federation Internationale de Football Association (FIFA) and is played every four years.

59

Soccer Player with the Highest Salary

David Beckham

Soccer Players with the
HIGHEST SALARIES

Annual salaries,
in millions of US dollars

David Beckham, Real Madrid	Zinedine Zidane, Real Madrid	Cristiano Ronaldo, Real Madrid	Rio Ferdinand, Manchester United	Alessandro Del Piero, Juventus
$16.9 M	$15.8 M	$13.2 M	$10.9 M	$10.8 M

David Beckham, a midfielder for Real Madrid, earned $16.9 million in 2005. Beckham began his career with England's Manchester United in 1996, and was named Young Player of the Year the following year. He played in the 1996 and 1999 English Cups and the 1999 Intercontinental Cup. Beckham was later named Manchester United's team captain in 2000. In July 2003, Beckham signed with Real Madrid. In addition to his salary, he has also made more than $20 million on endorsement deals.

Woman with the
Most CAPS

Kristine Lilly

With a total of 302, Kristine Lilly holds the world record for the most CAPS, or international games played. This is the highest number of CAPS in both the men's and women's international soccer organizations. Lilly has played more than 23,000 minutes—that's 383 hours—for the U.S. National Team. In 2004, Lilly scored her 100th international goal, becoming only one of five women to ever accomplish that. In 2005, Lilly was named U.S. Soccer's Female Athlete of the Year.

Women with the
MOST CAPS

Career CAPS

302	275	271	239	204
Kristine Lilly, USA, 1987–	Mia Hamm, USA, 1987–2004	Julie Foudy, USA, 1988–2004	Joy Fawcett, USA, 1987–2004	Tiffeny Milbrett, USA, 1991–2005

Team with the
Most Stanley Cup Wins

Montreal Canadiens

The Montreal Canadiens have won an amazing 24 Stanley Cup victories between 1916 and 1993. That's almost one-quarter of all the Stanley Cups ever played. The team plays at Montreal's Molson Centre. The Canadiens were created in December 1909 by J. Ambrose O'Brien to play for the National Hockey Association (NHA). They eventually made the transition into the National Hockey League. Over the years, the Canadiens have included such great players as Maurice Richard, George Hainsworth, Jacques Lemaire, Saku Koivu, and Emile Bouchard.

Team with the
MOST STANLEY CUP WINS

Stanley Cups won

24	11	10	5	5
Montreal Canadiens, 1916–1993	Toronto Maple Leafs, 1932–1967	Detroit Red Wings, 1936–2002	Boston Bruins, 1929–1972	Edmonton Oilers, 1984–1990

Montreal Canadiens with Stanley Cup

Most Career
Points

Wayne Gretzky

Wayne Gretzky scored an unbelievable 2,857 points and 894 goals during his 20-year career. Gretzky was the first person in the NHL to average more than two points per game. Many people consider Canadian-born Gretzky to be the greatest player in the history of the National Hockey League. In fact, he is called the "Great One." He officially retired from the sport in 1999 and was inducted into the Hockey Hall of Fame that same year. After his final game, the NHL retired his jersey number (99). In 2005, Gretzky became the head coach of the Phoenix Coyotes.

Players Who Scored the
MOST CAREER POINTS

Points scored

Wayne Gretzky, 1979–1999	Mark Messier, 1979–2004	Gordie Howe, 1954–1980	Ron Francis, 1981–2004	Marcel Dionne, 1971–1990
2,857	1,887	1,850	1,798	1,771

Goalie with the
Most Career Wins

Patrick Roy

During his 20 years in the NHL, Patrick Roy won 551 games. Roy also holds the NHL records for most 30-or-more win seasons (11), most playoff games played (240), most playoff minutes played (14,783), and most playoff wins (148). He was also a member of the Montreal Canadiens when they won the Stanley Cup in 1986 and 1993. Roy helped his team—the Colorado Avalanche—to win the Stanley Cup Championships in 1996 and 2001. On May 29, 2003, Roy announced his retirement from the sport.

Goaltenders with the
MOST CAREER WINS

Games won

Patrick Roy, 1984–2003	Terry Sawchuck, 1945–1970	Jacques Plante, 1951–1975	Ed Belfour, 1988–	Tony Esposito, 1963–1981
551	447	437	435	423

World's
Most Valuable Hockey Team

Toronto Maple Leafs

The Toronto Maple Leafs are worth an astounding $325 million, making them the most valuable hockey team in the world. This value is determined by assigning a monetary value to each of the team's players, based on their skills, performance, and contract value. Formerly known as the Toronto Arenas, the team was formed in 1917. Ten years later, the team changed to its current name. The Leafs have won 13 Stanley Cups between 1918 and 1967. Some of the most famous players associated with the team include Turk Broda, Tim Horton, Syl Apps, Darryl Sittler, and Ed Belfour. The team's home ice is at the Air Canada Centre.

The World's
MOST VALUABLE HOCKEY TEAMS

Team value, in millions of US dollars

Toronto Maple Leafs	New York Rangers	Philadelphia Flyers	Dallas Stars	Detroit Red Wings
$325 M	$282 M	$264 M	$259 M	$248 M

Driver with the Fastest
Daytona 500 Win

Buddy Baker

Race car legend Buddy Baker dominated the competition at the 1980 Daytona 500 with a top average speed of 177 miles (285 km) per hour. It was the first Daytona 500 race run under three hours. Baker had a history of speed before this race—he became the first driver to race more than 200 miles (322 km) on a closed course in 1970. During his amazing career, Baker competed in 688 Winston Cup races—he won 19 of them and finished in the top five in 198 others. He also won more than $3.6 million. He was inducted into the International Motorsports Hall of Fame in 1997.

Drivers with the
FASTEST DAYTONA 500 WINS
Average miles/kilometers per hour

177.60 mph/ 285.82 kph	176.26 mph/ 283.66 kph	172.71 mph/ 277.95 kph	172.26 mph/ 277.23 kph	169.65 mph/ 273.03 kph
Buddy Baker, 1980	Bill Elliott, 1987	Dale Earnhardt, 1998	Bill Elliott, 1985	Richard Petty, 1981

66

Driver with the
Fastest Indianapolis 500 Win

In 1990, race car driver Arie Luyendyk won the Indianapolis 500 with an average speed of 186 miles (299 km) per hour—the fastest average speed ever recorded in the history of the race. This was the first Indy 500 race for Luyendyk, and he drove a Lola/Chevy Indy V8 as part of the Shierson Racing team. In 1997, Luyendyk had another Indy 500 victory with an average speed of 146 miles (235 km) per hour. He also holds the record for the fastest Indy 500 practice lap at a speed of 239 miles (385 km) per hour.

Arie Luyendyk

Drivers with the
FASTEST INDIANAPOLIS 500 WINS
Speed in miles/kilometers per hour

185.98 mph/ 299.30 kph	176.45 mph/ 283.98 kph	170.72 mph/ 274.75 kph	167.61 mph/ 269.73 kph	167.58 mph/ 269.73 kph
Arie Luyendyk, 1990	Rick Mears, 1991	Bobby Rahal, 1986	Juan-Pablo Montoya, 2000	Emerson Fittipaldi, 1989

NASCAR Driver with the
Highest Career Earnings

Jeff Gordon

Jeff Gordon has won more than $74 million since he began racing in 1991. In fact, he was the first driver in history to earn more than $50 million. To date, Gordon has won four Winston Cup titles, three Daytona 500 titles, and 73 NASCAR Cup victories. His first Daytona 500 win in 1997 came when he was just 25 years old, making him the race's youngest winner. Gordon has competed in more than 400 NASCAR races and finished in the top-10 almost 65% of the time. He has raced for Hendrick Motorsports since 1992, and is part owner in the business.

NASCAR Drivers with the
HIGHEST CAREER EARNINGS

Career earnings,
in millions of US dollars

Jeff Gordon	Mark Martin	Dale Jarrett	Rusty Wallace	Tony Stewart
$74.8 M	$53.9 M	$52.3 M	$49.7 M	$48.5 M

Human-Made Records

Transportation • Constructions • Travel

Country with the
Most Cars

United States

The Countries with the
MOST CARS

Number of cars, in millions

USA	Japan	Germany	Italy	France
136.4 M	62.7 M	47.9 M	34.1 M	29.3 M

With more than 136 million cars registered in the United States, America outnumbers every country in the world in car ownership. This means that for every two Americans there is one car. That figure doesn't even include all of the trucks, campers, and motorcycles in the country. More than 90% of all U.S. residents have access to motor vehicles. With 18.9 million cars, California is the state with the most registered automobiles in the nation. Each year, U.S. drivers total about 4.2 trillion passenger miles (6.8 million passenger km) of travel and burn about 200 billion gallons (757 billion l) of fuel. The average American driver also spends about 21 hours each year stuck in traffic.

City with the World's
Longest Subway System

London

The world's longest subway system runs for 253 miles (408 km) below the streets of London. The London Underground—or tube as it's known by the locals—carries about 976 million people each year. The city's first underground railroad opened in 1863, and today it operates 500 peak trains and 275 stations. The subway's busiest station is Waterloo, which serves about 46,000 commuters during the morning rush. Throughout the subway system, some 412 escalators and 112 elevators keep commuter traffic moving.

The Cities with the World's
LONGEST SUBWAY SYSTEMS

Subway length in miles/kilometers

253 mi. 408 km.	231 mi. 372 km.	163 mi. 262 km.	160 mi. 258 km.	126 mi. 203 km.
London	New York	Moscow	Tokyo	Paris

City with the Busiest Subway System

Moscow

The World's Busiest
SUBWAY SYSTEMS
Passengers per year, in billions

Moscow	Tokyo	Seoul	Mexico City	New York City
3.28 B	2.91 B	2.42 B	1.67 B	1.40 B

Moscow's bustling Metropolitan (Metro) subway system transports more than 3 billion people each year. It is not only busy, it is also world renowned for its beautiful architecture. Many of the 150 stations have stained glass, marble statuary, and sparkling chandeliers. The rail network is 153 miles (246 km) long and follows the street pattern above. About half of the subway riders travel for free because they are students, retirees, police officers, or military personnel. Other riders pay 7 rubles, or about 25 cents, per ride.

Country with the
Most Roads

The United States

The Countries with the
MOST ROADS

Miles/kilometers of roads

3,972,801 mi. 6,393,603 km.	2,393,173 mi. 3,851,440 km.	1,124,575 mi. 1,809,829 km.	1,071,821 mi. 1,724,929 km.	731,526 mi. 1,177,278 km.
USA	India	China	Brazil	Japan

The United States is connected by a system of roads that measures 3,972,801 miles (6,393,603 km). Approximately 2.6 million miles (4.2 million km) of these roads are paved. About three-quarters of the roads, or 2.9 million miles (4.7 million km), are part of the national road system. Each person in America makes an average of four outings and travels some 47 miles (75 km) each day. Because Americans are always on the move, it's not surprising that the nation's highways are frequently tied up with traffic jams. Americans waste about 7 billion gallons (26.5 billion l) of fuel and 4.3 billion hours annually because they are stuck in traffic.

73

World's Longest
Underwater Tunnel

Seikan Tunnel

At 33.4 miles (53.8 km) the Seikan Tunnel is both the longest railway tunnel and the longest underwater tunnel in the world. It connects Honshu—the main island of Japan—to Hokkaido, an island to the north. Some 14.3 miles (23 km) of the tunnel run under the Tsugaru Strait, which connects the Pacific Ocean to the Sea of Japan. A railway in the tunnel transports passengers. Construction began in 1964 and took 24 years to complete at a cost of $7 billion. Today, the Seikan Tunnel is no longer the quickest way between the two islands. Air travel is faster and almost the same price.

The World's
LONGEST UNDERWATER TUNNELS

Length in miles/kilometers

33.4 mi. 53.8 km.	31.0 mi. 49.9 km.	13.8 mi. 22.2 km.	11.6 mi. 18.8 km.	5.0 mi. 9.5 km.
Seikan Tunnel, Japan	Channel Tunnel, France/England	Dai-Shimizu Tunnel, Japan	Shin-Kanmon Tunnel, Japan	Tokyo Bay Aqualine, Japan

World's Longest Road Tunnel

Laerdal

The Laerdal Tunnel was officially opened in Norway on November 27, 2000 and measures 15.2 miles (24.5 km). This huge construction makes its way under large mountain chains to connect the capital, Oslo, to the port of Bergen, Norway's second-largest city. The tunnel is 29.5 feet (9 m) wide and 21 feet (6.3 m) high. It is estimated that about 1,000 cars and trucks make the 20-minute drive through the tunnel each day. To help make the tunnel safe, the designers installed special lighting to keep drivers alert. There are also turning areas in case drivers need to stop. The tunnels are equipped with state-of-the-art ventilation systems and special signal boosters that allow cell phone reception.

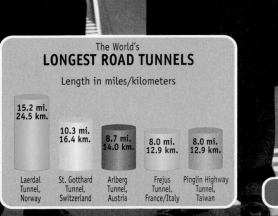

The World's
LONGEST ROAD TUNNELS

Length in miles/kilometers

15.2 mi. 24.5 km.	10.3 mi. 16.4 km.	8.7 mi. 14.0 km.	8.0 mi. 12.9 km.	8.0 mi. 12.9 km.
Laerdal Tunnel, Norway	St. Gotthard Tunnel, Switzerland	Arlberg Tunnel, Austria	Frejus Tunnel, France/Italy	Pinglin Highway Tunnel, Taiwan

World's
Highest City

Wenchuan, China

Sitting 16,730 feet (5,099 m) above the sea, Wenchuan, China, is the world's highest city. That's 3.2 miles (5.2 km) high, more than half the height of Mt. Everest. There are several ancient villages in the area with houses dating back hundreds of years. Located nearby is the Wolong Panda Preserve—one of the last places on Earth where the endangered bears are studied and bred. The city is part of the Sichuan Province, which is located in southwest China. The province covers 207,340 square miles (537,000 sq km) and has a population of 103.2 million.

The World's
HIGHEST CITIES

Height above sea level
in feet/meters

16,730 ft. 5,099 m.	13,045 ft. 3,976 m.	12,146 ft. 3,702 m.	12,087 ft. 3,684 m.	11,916 ft. 3,632 m.
Wenchuan, China	Potosi, Bolivia	Oruro, Bolivia	Lhasa, Tibet	La Paz, Bolivia

World's
Longest Ship Canal

Grand Canal

The World's
LONGEST SHIP CANALS

Length in miles/kilometers

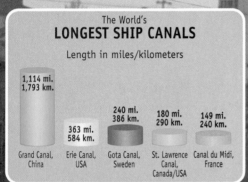

1,114 mi. 1,793 km.	363 mi. 584 km.	240 mi. 386 km.	180 mi. 290 km.	149 mi. 240 km.
Grand Canal, China	Erie Canal, USA	Gota Canal, Sweden	St. Lawrence Canal, Canada/USA	Canal du Midi, France

The Grand Canal flows for 1,114 miles (1,793 km) through China, connecting Beijing to Hangzhou. The canal measures between 100 and 200 feet (30 and 60 m) wide and between 2 and 15 feet (0.6 and 4.6 m) deep. There are 24 locks and 60 bridges along the Grand Canal. Construction on the canal began in the sixth century BC and continued for 2,000 years. Since most of China's main rivers flow from west to east, the north-and-south flowing canal is an important connection between the Yangtze River valley and the Yellow River valley.

World's Largest Mall

South China Mall

The South China Mall in Dongguan City is a shopper's paradise with 7.1 million square feet (0.66 M sq m) of retail and entertainment space. There are 11 large anchor stores, and 1,500 smaller shops. The megamall—which opened in 2005—was designed with seven major areas that are designed to resemble Amsterdam, Paris, Rome, Venice, Egypt, the Caribbean, and California. And, for shoppers too tired to walk from one end of the giant retail outlet to the other, there are gondolas and water taxis located on the one-mile, human-made canal that circles the perimeter.

The World's LARGEST MALLS

Area in millions of square feet/square meters

7.1 M sq. ft. 0.66 M sq. m.	South China Mall, China
6.0 M sq. ft. 0.56 M sq. m.	Golden Resources Shopping Mall, China
5.3 M sq. ft. 0.49 M sq. m.	West Edmonton Mall, Canada
4.7 M sq. ft. 0.44 M sq. m.	Beijing Mall, China
4.2 M sq. ft. 0.39 M sq. m.	Mall of America, Minnesota, USA

Amusement Park with the
Most Rides

Cedar Point

Located in Sandusky, Ohio, Cedar Point offers park visitors 68 rides to enjoy. Top Thrill Dragster—the park's newest roller coaster—is the tallest in the world at 420 feet (128 m). Another tall ride—the 300-foot (91 m) Power Tower—blasts riders up and down the towers at a speed of 55 miles (89 km) per hour. And with 16 roller coasters, Cedar Point also has the most coasters of any theme park in the world. Over 44,500 feet (13,564 m) of coaster track—more than 6 miles (9.7 km)—run through the park. Cedar Point opened in 1870 and is the second-oldest amusement park in the country.

The Amusement Parks with the
MOST RIDES

Number of rides

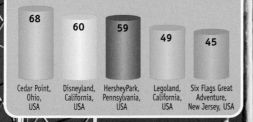

68	60	59	49	45
Cedar Point, Ohio, USA	Disneyland, California, USA	HersheyPark, Pennsylvania, USA	Legoland, California, USA	Six Flags Great Adventure, New Jersey, USA

City with the
Most Skyscrapers

New York City

New York City has 176 skyscrapers towering over its streets. At the mouth of the Hudson River in southeast New York State, New York City is an area of more than 308 square miles (797 sq km). A solid platform has made it possible for the island to support such large structures. Some of the city's tallest skyscrapers—such as the Empire State Building and the Chrysler Building—are world famous. Skyscrapers first became popular in the 1870s, when real estate prices in Manhattan made it more economical to build up instead of out.

World Cities with the
MOST SKYSCRAPERS
Number of skyscrapers

176	105	82	70	57
New York City, New York, USA	Hong Kong, China	Chicago, Illinois, USA	Shanghai, China	Tokyo, Japan

World's Tallest
Apartment Building

Q1, a new luxury apartment complex on Australia's Gold Coast, rises 1,058 feet (323 m) above the surrounding sand. There are 526 apartments within the building's 80 floors. Some apartments have glass-enclosed balconies. Q1 residents can enjoy Australia's only beachside observation deck and a 10-story sky garden. Some other amenities include retail outlets, a lagoon swimming pool, spa, sauna, and fitness center. And just in case all nine elevators are out of order, there are 1,430 steps from the penthouse to the basement.

The World's
TALLEST APARTMENT BUILDINGS

Height in feet/meters

1,058 ft. 323 m.	975 ft. 297 m.	863 ft. 263 m.	656 ft. 200 m.	645 ft. 197 m.
Q1, Gold Coast, Australia	Eureka Tower, Melbourne, Australia	Trump World Towers, New York, USA	Tregunter Tower III, Hong Kong, China	Lake Point Tower, Chicago, USA

World's
Largest Dome

Millennium Dome

The Millennium Dome has a roof that measures 1,050 feet (320 m) in diameter and covers 861,113 square feet (80,000 sq m). That's large enough to contain the Great Pyramid of Giza! The roof is made of 107,639 square feet (10,000 sq m) of fabric and is held up by 43 miles of steel cable. Located on the meridian line in Greenwich, England—the first spot to greet the new year—the dome was built for the country's millennium celebration. After the New Year's celebration, renovations began to turn the dome into a sports complex, and it will be used for the 2012 Olympics.

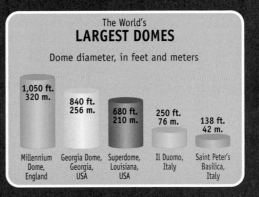

The World's
LARGEST DOMES
Dome diameter, in feet and meters

Millennium Dome, England	Georgia Dome, Georgia, USA	Superdome, Louisiana, USA	Il Duomo, Italy	Saint Peter's Basilica, Italy
1,050 ft. 320 m.	840 ft. 256 m.	680 ft. 210 m.	250 ft. 76 m.	138 ft. 42 m.

World's Tallest Habitable Building

Taipei 101

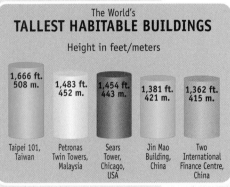

The World's
TALLEST HABITABLE BUILDINGS

Height in feet/meters

1,666 ft. 508 m.	1,483 ft. 452 m.	1,454 ft. 443 m.	1,381 ft. 421 m.	1,362 ft. 415 m.
Taipei 101, Taiwan	Petronas Twin Towers, Malaysia	Sears Tower, Chicago, USA	Jin Mao Building, China	Two International Finance Centre, China

Located in Taipei's Xinyi district, Taipei 101 towers over the city at a height of 1,666 feet (508 m). To reflect Taiwan's culture, the pagoda-style office building was designed to resemble sturdy bamboo stalks growing out of the ground. The 101-story building has 2.14 million square feet (198,348 sq m) of office space, and an additional 804,182 square feet (74,711 sq m) for a shopping center. As a safety precaution, the steel-frame building was built to withstand the country's strongest earthquakes and winds at a force of 134 miles (216 km) per hour.

World's Highest
Suspension Bridge

Royal Gorge

The World's
HIGHEST SUSPENSION BRIDGES

Height in feet/meters

1,053 ft. 321 m.	804 ft. 245 m.	507 ft. 155 m.	318 ft. 97 m.	228 ft. 69 m.
Royal Gorge, Colorado, USA	Viaduc de Millau, France	Tacoma Narrows, Washington, USA	Akashi-Kaikyo, Japan	Verrazano-Narrows, New York, USA

Located in Canon City, Colorado, the Royal Gorge Bridge spans the Arkansas River 1,053 feet (321 m) above the water. The bridge is 1,260 feet (384 m) long and 18 feet (5 m) wide. About 1,000 tons (907 t) of steel make up the bridge's floor, which can hold in excess of 2 million pounds (907,200 kg). The cables weigh about 300 tons (272 t) each. The bridge took just five months to complete in 1929, at a cost of $350,000.

World's Longest
Suspension Bridge

Akashi-Kaikyo

The Akashi-Kaikyo connects Maiko, Tarumi Ward, in Kobe City to Matsuho, Awaji Town, in Japan. All together, the suspension bridge spans the Akashi Strait for 2 miles (3 km) in Tsuna County on the Japanese island of Awajishima. Built in 1998, the structure's main span is a record-breaking 6,529 feet (1,990 m) long with cables supporting the 100,000-ton (90,700-t) bridge below. Each cable is made up of 290 strands of wire. The main tower soars approximately 984 feet (300 m) into the air. The bridge needed to be high above the water so it didn't block ships entering the Akashi Strait.

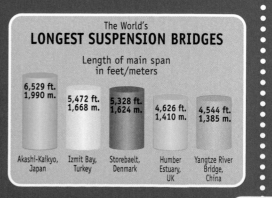

The World's
LONGEST SUSPENSION BRIDGES

Length of main span
in feet/meters

6,529 ft. 1,990 m.	5,472 ft. 1,668 m.	5,328 ft. 1,624 m.	4,626 ft. 1,410 m.	4,544 ft. 1,385 m.
Akashi-Kaikyo, Japan	Izmit Bay, Turkey	Storebaelt, Denmark	Humber Estuary, UK	Yangtze River Bridge, China

85

World's Most-Visited City

New York City

The World's
MOST-VISITED CITIES

Annual visitors, in millions

41.0 M	34.7 M	30.0 M	26.6 M	20.6 M
New York City, USA	Tijuana, Mexico	Paris, France	London, England	Hong Kong, China

In just one year, more than 41 million tourists visit New York City. That's the equivalent of the entire population of Canada coming for vacation! Both domestic and international travelers come to New York City to enjoy the theater and performing arts, museums, shopping, and historical landmarks. Collectively, visitors contribute more than $21 billion to the city's economy annually. Just more than 6.5 million tourists are from other countries, and most come from the United Kingdom, Canada, and Japan. During their stay, most travelers take advantage of the city's 70,545 hotel rooms and 17,312 restaurants.

World's Top
Tourist Country

France

The World's
TOP TOURIST COUNTRIES
International visitors, in millions

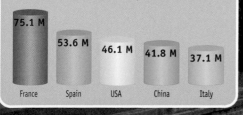

France	Spain	USA	China	Italy
75.1 M	53.6 M	46.1 M	41.8 M	37.1 M

France hosts more than 75 million tourists annually. That's more than twice the number of people living in all of New England combined. The most popular French destinations are Paris and the Mediterranean coast. In July and August—the most popular months to visit France—tourists flock to the westernmost coastal areas of the region. In the winter, visitors hit the slopes at major ski resorts in the northern Alps. Tourists also visit many of France's world-renowned landmarks and monuments, including the Eiffel Tower, Notre-Dame, the Louvre, and the Arc de Triomphe. Most tourists are from other European countries, especially Germany.

Country with the
Most Airports

United States

There are 14,857 airports located in the United States. That is more than the number of airports for the other nine top countries combined. The top two busiest airports in the world are also located in the United States. All together, U.S. airports serve more than 698 million travelers a year. With the threat of terrorism and the state of the economy, the airline industry lost $10 billion in 2002. In September 2005, rising fuel costs and competition from discount airlines caused several major airlines—including Delta and Northwest—to file for bankruptcy.

The Countries with the
MOST AIRPORTS

Number of airports

USA	Brazil	Russia	Mexico	Argentina
14,857	4,136	2,586	1,833	1,334

World's
Busiest Airport

Hartsfield Atlanta International Airport

The Hartsfield Atlanta International Airport served more than 83 million travelers in one year. That's more people than are living in California, Texas, and Florida combined. Approximately 2,200 planes depart and arrive at this airport every day. With parking lots, runways, maintenance facilities, and other buildings, the Hartsfield terminal complex covers about 130 acres (53 ha). Hartsfield Atlanta International Airport has a north and a south terminal, as well as an underground train, and six concourses that feature many shops, restaurants, and banks.

The World's BUSIEST AIRPORTS

Annual passengers, in millions

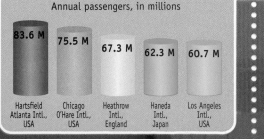

83.6 M	75.5 M	67.3 M	62.3 M	60.7 M
Hartsfield Atlanta Intl., USA	Chicago O'Hare Intl., USA	Heathrow Intl., England	Haneda Intl., Japan	Los Angeles Intl., USA

United States's Most-Visited National Site

Blue Ridge Parkway

The United States's
MOST-VISITED NATIONAL SITES

Annual visitors, in millions

17.99 M	13.27 M	9.17 M	8.22 M	7.82 M
Blue Ridge Parkway, North Carolina–Virginia	Golden Gate National Recreation Area, California	Great Smoky Mountains, Tennessee–North Carolina	Gateway National Recreation Area, New Jersey–New York	Lake Mead National Recreation Area, Arizona–Nevada

Each year nearly 18 million people travel to North Carolina and Virginia to visit the Blue Ridge Parkway. The Blue Ridge is part of the eastern Appalachian Mountains and has an average elevation of 3,000 feet (914 m). The 469-mile (755 km) stretch of road winds through four national forests. Construction began on the country's first scenic parkway in 1935, and was completed in 1987. Some of the most popular activities along the Blue Ridge Parkway include hiking, camping, bicycling, and photographing nature.

Nature Records

Animals • Natural Formations
Food • Weather • Plants • Disasters

World's Largest Crustacean

Giant Spider Crab

The giant spider crab has a 12-foot- (3.7-m-) wide leg span. That's almost wide enough to take up two parking spaces! The crab's body measures about 15 inches (38.1 cm) wide. Its ten long legs are jointed, and the first set has large claws at the end. The giant sea creature can weigh between 35 and 44 pounds (16 and 20 kg). It feeds on dead animals and shellfish it finds on the ocean floor. Giant spider crabs live in the deep water of the Pacific Ocean off southern Japan.

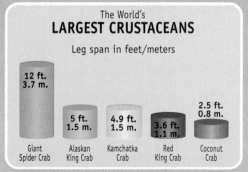

The World's
LARGEST CRUSTACEANS

Leg span in feet/meters

Giant Spider Crab	Alaskan King Crab	Kamchatka Crab	Red King Crab	Coconut Crab
12 ft. 3.7 m.	5 ft. 1.5 m.	4.9 ft. 1.5 m.	3.6 ft. 1.1 m.	2.5 ft. 0.8 m.

World's
Loudest Animal

Blue Whale

The World's
LOUDEST ANIMALS
In decibels

Blue Whale	Sperm Whale	Dolphin	Fin Whale	Manatee
188	170	165	160	100

The loudest animal on Earth is the blue whale. The giant mammal's call can reach up to 188 decibels—about 40 decibels louder than a jet engine. The rumbling, low-frequency sounds of the blue whale can travel several miles underwater. The whale's whistling call can be heard for several hundred miles below the sea. Much of this whale chatter is used for communication, especially during the mating season. People cannot detect the whales' calls, however, because they are too low-pitched for humans' ears.

World's
Biggest Fish

Whale Shark

The World's
BIGGEST FISH

Average weight in pounds/kilograms

Whale Shark	Basking Shark	Great White Shark	Greenland Shark	Tiger Shark
50,000 lb. 22,680 kg.	32,000 lb. 14,515 kg.	7,000 lb. 3,175 kg.	2,250 lb. 1,020 kg.	2,070 lb. 939 kg.

Although the average length of a whale shark is 30 feet (9 m), many have been known to reach up to 60 feet (18 m) long. That's the same length as two school buses! Whale sharks also weigh an average of 50,000 pounds (22,680 kg). As with most sharks, the females are larger than the males. Their mouths measure about 5 feet (1.5 m) long and contain about 3,000 teeth. Amazingly, these gigantic fish eat only microscopic plankton and tiny fish. They float near the surface looking for food.

World's Largest Pinniped

Southern Elephant Seal

The World's
LARGEST PINNIPEDS

Length in feet/meters

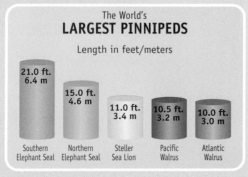

Southern Elephant Seal	Northern Elephant Seal	Steller Sea Lion	Pacific Walrus	Atlantic Walrus
21.0 ft. 6.4 m	15.0 ft. 4.6 m	11.0 ft. 3.4 m	10.5 ft. 3.2 m	10.0 ft. 3.0 m

The southern elephant seal is the largest member of the seal and sea lion family (or pinnipeds), with bulls (males) measuring more than 21 feet (6.4 m) long and weighing up to 8,800 pounds (3,992 kg). This giant pinniped got its name from its long nose that resembles an elephant's trunk. Southern elephant seals are also amazing divers and can reach depths of 3,280 feet (1,000 m) for up to 2 hours. These smart animals are very social and live in large groups. Their largest colonies are found around South Georgia and Macquarie Island.

World's
Slowest Fish

Sea Horse

With a speed of just .001 miles (.002 km) per hour, sea horses don't get anywhere fast. At that rate of speed, it would take the fish about an hour to swim only 5 feet (1.5 m). They range in size from less than half an inch (1 cm) to almost 1 foot (0.3 m). Sea horses spend most of their time near the shore. There, they can hold on to plants with their tails. This helps them avoid enemies. Approximately 50 different species of sea horses are found throughout the world. However, due to overharvesting, the sea horse population has decreased by up to 95%.

Some of the World's
SLOWEST FISH

Average speed in miles/kilometers

Sea Horse	Barracuda	Tiger Shark	Tarpon	Swordfish
.001 mph .002 kph	25 mph 40 kph	33 mph 53 kph	35 mph 56 kph	40 mph 64 kph

World's Fastest Fish

Sailfish

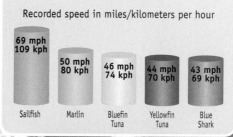

The World's
FASTEST FISH

Recorded speed in miles/kilometers per hour

Sailfish	Marlin	Bluefin Tuna	Yellowfin Tuna	Blue Shark
69 mph 109 kph	50 mph 80 kph	46 mph 74 kph	44 mph 70 kph	43 mph 69 kph

A sailfish once grabbed a fishing line and dragged it 300 feet (91 m) away in just 3 seconds. That means it was swimming at an average speed of 69 miles (109 km) per hour—just higher than the average speed limit on the highway! Sailfish are very large—they average 6 feet (1.8 m) long, but can grow up to 11 feet (3.4 m). Sailfish eat squid and surface-dwelling fish. Sometimes several sailfish will work together to catch their prey. They are found in both the Atlantic and Pacific oceans and prefer a water temperature of about 80°F (27°C).

World's Largest
Bird Wingspan

Marabou Stork

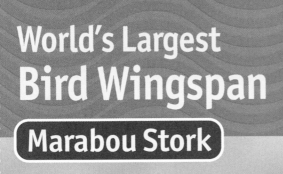

With a wingspan that can reach up to 13 feet (4 m), the Marabou stork has the largest wingspan of any bird. These large storks weigh up to 20 pounds (9 kg) and can grow up to 5 feet (150 cm) tall. Their long leg and toe bones are actually hollow. This adaptation is very important for flight because it makes the bird lighter. Although marabous eat insects, small mammals, and fish, the majority of their food is carrion—already-dead meat. In fact, the stork's head and neck do not have any feathers. This helps the bird stay clean as it sticks its head into carcasses to pick out scraps of food.

The World's
LARGEST BIRD WINGSPANS

Wingspan in feet/meters

Marabou Stork	Albatross	Trumpeter Swan	Mute Swan	Whooper Swan
13 ft. 4 m.	12 ft. 3.7 m.	11 ft. 3.4 m.	10 ft. 3 m.	10 ft. 3 m.

World's
Fastest Flyer

Peregrine Falcon

A peregrine falcon can reach speeds of up to 175 miles (282 km) an hour while diving through the air. That's about the same speed as the fastest race car in the Indianapolis 500. These powerful birds can catch prey in midair and kill it instantly with their sharp claws. Peregrine falcons range from about 13 to 19 inches (33 to 48 cm) long. The female is called a falcon, but the male is called a tercel, which means "one-third" in German. This is because the male is about one-third the size of the female.

The World's
FASTEST FLYERS

Top speed in miles/kilometers per hour

175 mph 282 kph	106 mph 171 kph	95 mph 153 kph	88 mph 142 kph	80 mph 129 kph
Peregrine Falcon	Spine-tailed Swift	Frigate Bird	Spur-winged Goose	Red-breasted Merganser

World's Longest Bird Migration

Arctic Tern

The World's
LONGEST BIRD MIGRATIONS
Round-trip migration in miles/kilometers

Bird	Miles	Kilometers
Arctic Tern	22,000 mi.	35,406 km.
White-rumped Sandpiper	20,000 mi.	32,187 km.
Red Knot	20,000 mi.	32,187 km.
Lesser Yellowleg	18,000 mi.	28,968 km.
Swainson's Hawk	15,000 mi.	24,140 km.

The arctic tern migrates from Maine to the coast of Africa, and then on to Antarctica, flying some 22,000 miles (35,406 km) a year. That's almost the same measurement as the Earth's circumference. Some don't complete the journey however—young terns fly the first half of the journey with parents, but remain in Antarctica for a year or two. When they have matured, the birds fly back to Maine and the surrounding areas. Scientists are puzzled by how these birds remember the way back after only making the journey once so early in their lives.

Bird That Builds the Largest Nest

With a nest that can measure 8 feet (2.4 m) wide and 16 feet (4.9 m) deep, bald eagles have plently of room to move around. These birds of prey have wingspans of up to 7.5 feet (2.3 m) and need a home that they can nest in comfortably. By carefully constructing their nest with sticks, branches, and plant material, a pair of bald eagles can balance their home—which can weigh up to 4,000 pounds (8,800 kg)—on the top of a tree or cliff. These nests are usually located by rivers or coastlines, the birds' watery hunting grounds. Called an aerie, this home will be used for the rest of the eagles' lives.

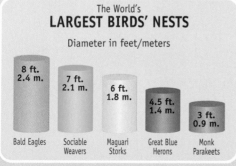

The World's
LARGEST BIRDS' NESTS

Diameter in feet/meters

8 ft. 2.4 m.	7 ft. 2.1 m.	6 ft. 1.8 m.	4.5 ft. 1.4 m.	3 ft. 0.9 m.
Bald Eagles	Sociable Weavers	Maguari Storks	Great Blue Herons	Monk Parakeets

World's Largest Bird Egg

Ostrich Egg

Ostriches—the world's largest birds—can lay eggs that measure 5 inches by 6 inches (13 cm by 16 cm) and weigh up to 4 pounds (1.8 kg). In fact, just one ostrich egg equals up to 24 chicken eggs. The egg yolk makes up one-third of the volume. Although the egg shell is only .08 inch (2 mm) thick, it is tough enough to withstand the weight of a 345-pound (157-kg) ostrich. A hen ostrich can lay from 10 to 70 eggs each year. Females are usually able to recognize their own eggs, even when they are mixed in with those of other females in their shared nest.

The World's
LARGEST BIRD EGGS

Weight of egg in pounds/kilograms

4.0 lb. 1.8 kg.	1.8 lb. 0.82 kg.	1.6 lb. 0.72 kg.	1.5 lb. 0.68 kg.	1.0 lb. 0.45 kg.
Ostrich	Emu	Kiwi	Emperor Penguin	Albatross

World's
Fastest Land Bird

Ostrich

An ostrich can run at a top speed of 45 miles (72.4 km) per hour for about 30 minutes. This allows the speedy bird to easily outrun most predators. Its long, powerful legs help an ostrich cover 10 to 15 feet (3.1 to 4.6 km) per bound. And although it is a flightless bird, an ostrich uses it wings for balance when it runs. If an ostrich does need to defend itself, it has a kick powerful enough to kill a lion. The ostrich, which is also the world's largest bird at 10 feet (3.1 m) tall and 350 pounds (158.8 kg), is native to the savannas of Africa.

The World's
FASTEST LAND BIRDS

Speed in miles/kilometers per hour

45 mph 72.4 kph	40 mph 64.4 kph	20 mph 32.2 kph	17 mph 27.4 kph	15 mph 24.1 kph
Ostrich	Emu	Wild Turkey	Roadrunner	Yellow-billed Cuckoo

World's Fastest Shark

Mako Shark

A mako shark can cruise through the water at 50 miles (79.4 km) per hour—about the speed limit of most highways. This super speed helps the shark catch its food, which consists mostly of tuna, herring, mackerel, swordfish, and porpoise. Occasionally makos even build up enough speed to leap out of the water. Mako sharks average 7 feet (2.1 m) in length, but can grow up to 12 feet (3.7 m) and weigh 1,000 pounds (454 kg). The sharks are found in temperate and tropical seas throughout the world.

The World's
FASTEST SHARKS

Fastest speed in
miles/kilometers per hour

50 mph 79.4 kph	43 mph 69.2 kph	25 mph 40.2 kph	22 mph 35.4 kph	20 mph 32.2 kph
Mako Shark	Blue Shark	Great White Shark	Tiger Shark	Lemon Shark

World's Heaviest
Marine Mammal

Blue Whale

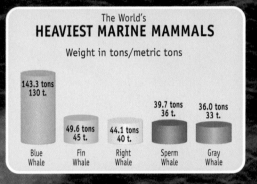

The World's
HEAVIEST MARINE MAMMALS

Weight in tons/metric tons

143.3 tons 130 t.	49.6 tons 45 t.	44.1 tons 40 t.	39.7 tons 36 t.	36.0 tons 33 t.
Blue Whale	Fin Whale	Right Whale	Sperm Whale	Gray Whale

Blue whales are the largest animals that have ever inhabited earth. They can weigh more than 143.3 tons (130 t) and measure over 100 feet (30 m) long. Amazingly, these gentle giants only eat krill—small, shrimplike animals. A blue whale can eat about 4 tons (3.6 t) of krill each day in the summer, when food is plentiful . To catch the krill, a whale gulps as much as 17,000 gallons (64,600 l) of seawater into its mouth at one time. Then it uses its tongue—which can be the same size as a car—to push the water back out. The krill get caught in hairs on the whale's baleen (a keratin structure that hangs down from the roof of the whale's mouth).

World's Heaviest Land Mammal

African Elephant

Weighing in at up to 14,430 pounds (6,545 kg) and measuring approximately 24 feet (7.3 m) long, African elephants are truly humongous. Even at their great size, they are strictly vegetarian. They will, however, eat up to 500 pounds (226 kg) of vegetation a day! Their two tusks—which are really elongated teeth—grow continuously during their lives and can reach about 9 feet (2.7 m) in length. Elephants live in small groups of 8 to 15 family members with one female (called a cow) as the leader.

The World's
HEAVIEST LAND MAMMALS

In pounds/kilograms

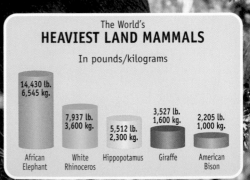

African Elephant	White Rhinoceros	Hippopotamus	Giraffe	American Bison
14,430 lb. 6,545 kg.	7,937 lb. 3,600 kg.	5,512 lb. 2,300 kg.	3,527 lb. 1,600 kg.	2,205 lb. 1,000 kg.

World's
Largest Rodent
Capybara

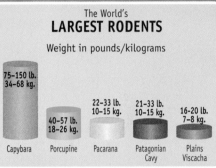

The World's
LARGEST RODENTS
Weight in pounds/kilograms

75–150 lb.
34–68 kg.

40–57 lb.
18–26 kg.

22–33 lb.
10–15 kg.

21–33 lb.
10–15 kg.

16–20 lb.
7–8 kg.

Capybara   Porcupine   Pacarana   Patagonian   Plains
                                      Cavy   Viscacha

Capybaras reach an average length of 4 feet (1.2 m), stand about 20 inches (51 cm) tall, and weigh between 75 and 150 pounds (34 to 68 kg)! That's about the same size as a Labrador retriever. Also known as water hogs and carpinchos, capybaras are found in South and Central America, where they spend much of their time in groups looking for food. They are strictly vegetarian and have been known to raid gardens for melons and squash. Their partially webbed feet make capybaras excellent swimmers. They can dive down to the bottom of a lake or river to find plants and stay there for up to five minutes.

World's
Slowest Land Mammal

Three-toed Sloth

A three-toed sloth can reach a top speed of only .07 miles (.11 km) per hour while traveling on the ground. That means that it would take the animal almost 15 minutes to cross a four-lane street. The main reason sloths move so slowly is that they cannot walk like other mammals. They must pull themselves along the ground using only their sharp claws. Because of this, sloths spend the majority of their time in trees. There, they will sleep up to 18 hours each day. When they wake at night, they search for leaves and shoots to eat.

Some of the World's
SLOWEST LAND MAMMALS

Maximum speed in miles/kilometers per hour

Three-toed Sloth	Koala	Gibbon	Pig	Squirrel
.07 mph .11 kph	7 mph 11.3 kph	10 mph 16.1 kph	11 mph 18 kph	12 mph 19 kph

World's Fastest Land Mammal

Cheetah

The World's
FASTEST LAND MAMMALS

Maximum speed in
miles/kilometers per hour

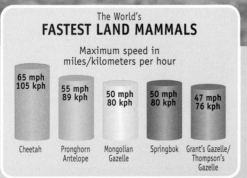

65 mph 105 kph	55 mph 89 kph	50 mph 80 kph	50 mph 80 kph	47 mph 76 kph
Cheetah	Pronghorn Antelope	Mongolian Gazelle	Springbok	Grant's Gazelle/ Thompson's Gazelle

For short spurts these sleek mammals can reach a speed of 65 miles (105 km) per hour. They can accelerate from 0 to 40 miles (64 km) per hour in just three strides. Their quickness easily enables these large African cats to outrun their prey. All other African cats must stalk their prey because they lack the cheetah's amazing speed. Unlike the paws of all other cats, cheetah paws do not have skin sheaths (thin protective coverings). Their claws, therefore, cannot pull back.

109

World's Tallest
Land Animal

Giraffe

Giraffes are the giants among mammals, growing to more than 18 feet (5.5 m) in height. That means an average giraffe could look through the window of a two-story building. A giraffe's neck is 18 times longer than a human's, but both mammals have exactly the same number of neck bones. A giraffe's long legs enable it to outrun most of its enemies. When cornered, a giraffe has been known to kill a lion with a single kick.

Some of the World's
TALLEST ANIMALS

Height in feet/meters

Giraffe	African Elephant	Camel	Moose	Rhino
18 ft. 5.5 m.	7 ft. 2 m.	6.5 ft. 2 m.	6 ft. 1.8 m.	5 ft. 1.5 m.

World's Largest Bat

Giant Flying Fox

A giant flying fox—a member of the megabat family—can have a wingspan of up to 6 feet (2 m). These furry mammals average just 7 wing beats per second, but can travel more than 40 miles (64 km) a night in search of food. Unlike smaller bats, flying foxes rely on their acute vision and sense of smell to locate fruit, pollen, and nectar. Flying foxes got their name because their faces resemble a fox's face. Megabats live in the tropical areas of Africa, Asia, and Australia.

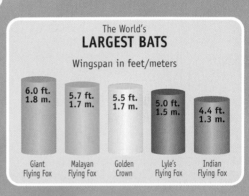

The World's
LARGEST BATS

Wingspan in feet/meters

Giant Flying Fox	Malayan Flying Fox	Golden Crown	Lyle's Flying Fox	Indian Flying Fox
6.0 ft. 1.8 m.	5.7 ft. 1.7 m.	5.5 ft. 1.7 m.	5.0 ft. 1.5 m.	4.4 ft. 1.3 m.

World's Most
Deadly Amphibian

Poison Dart Frog

Poison dart frogs are found mostly in the tropical rain forests of Central and South America, where they live on the moist land. These lethal amphibians have enough poison to kill up to 20 adults. A dart frog's poison is so effective that native Central and South Americans sometimes coat their hunting arrows or hunting darts with it. These brightly colored frogs can be yellow, orange, red, green, blue, or any combination of these colors and measure only .5 to 2 inches (1 to 5 cm) long. There are approximately 75 different species of poison dart frogs.

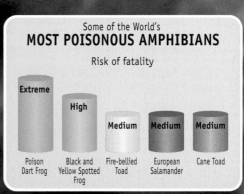

Some of the World's
MOST POISONOUS AMPHIBIANS

Risk of fatality

| Extreme | High | Medium | Medium | Medium |
| Poison Dart Frog | Black and Yellow Spotted Frog | Fire-bellied Toad | European Salamander | Cane Toad |

World's Longest Snake

Reticulated Python

Some adult reticulated pythons can grow to 27 feet (8.2 m) long, but most reach an average length of 17 feet (5 m). That's almost the length of an average school bus. These pythons live mostly in Asia, from Myanmar to Indonesia to the Philippines. The python has teeth that curve backward and can hold the snake's prey still. It hunts mainly at night and will eat mammals and birds. Reticulated pythons are slow-moving creatures that kill their prey by constriction, or strangulation.

The World's
LONGEST SNAKES

Length in feet/meters

27.0 ft. 8.2 m.	25.0 ft. 7.6 m.	24.6 ft. 7.5 m.	17.7 ft. 5.4 m.	12.2 ft. 3.7 m.
Reticulated Python	Anaconda	Rock Python	King Cobra	Oriental Rat Snake

Snake with the Longest Fangs

Gaboon Viper

The fangs of a Gaboon viper measure 2 inches (5 cm) in length! These giant fangs fold up against the snake's mouth so it does not pierce its own skin. When it is ready to strike its prey, the fangs snap down into position. The snake can grow up to 7 feet (2 m) long and weigh 18 pounds (8 kg). It is found in Africa and is perfectly camouflaged for hunting on the ground beneath leaves and grasses. The Gaboon viper's poison is not as toxic as some other snakes, but it is quite dangerous because of the amount of poison it can inject at one time. The snake is not very aggressive, however, and usually only attacks when bothered.

Snakes with the
LONGEST FANGS

Fang length in inches/centimeters

Gaboon Viper	Bushmaster	Black Mamba	Diamondback Rattlesnake	Australian Taipan
2.0 in. 5.1 cm.	1.5 in. 3.8 cm.	1.0 in. 2.5 cm.	1.0 in. 2.5 cm.	0.7 in. 1.8 cm.

World's Deadliest Snake

Black Mamba

The World's
DEADLIEST SNAKES

Deaths possible per bite

Black Mamba	Taipan	Russell's Viper	Common Krait	Forest Cobra
200	170	150	60	50

With just one bite, an African black mamba snake releases a venom powerful enough to kill up to 200 humans. A bite from this snake is almost always fatal if it is not treated immediately. This large member of the cobra family grows to about 14 feet (4.3 m) long. In addition to its deadly poison, it is also a very aggressive snake. It will raise its body off the ground when it feels threatened. It then spreads its hood and strikes swiftly at its prey with its long front teeth.

A black mamba is also very fast—it can move along at about 7 miles (11.7 km) per hour for short bursts.

World's
Largest Amphibian

Chinese Giant Salamander

The World's
LARGEST AMPHIBIANS

Size in feet/meters

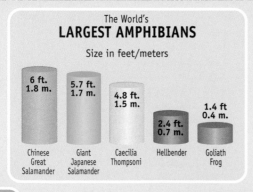

6 ft. 1.8 m.	5.7 ft. 1.7 m.	4.8 ft. 1.5 m.	2.4 ft. 0.7 m.	1.4 ft 0.4 m.
Chinese Great Salamander	Giant Japanese Salamander	Caecilia Thompsoni	Hellbender	Goliath Frog

With a length of 6 feet (1.8 m) and a weight of 55 pounds (25 kg), Chinese giant salamanders rule the amphibian world. This amphibian has a large head, but its eyes and nostrils are small. It has short legs, a long tail, and very smooth skin. This large amphibian can be found in the streams of northeastern, central, and southern China. It feeds on fish, frogs, crabs, and snakes. The giant Chinese salamander will not hunt its prey. It will wait until a potential meal wanders too close and then grab it in its mouth. Because many people enjoy the taste of the salamander's meat, it is often hunted and its population is shrinking.

World's Longest-Lived
Reptile

Galápagos Tortoise

The World's
LONGEST-LIVED REPTILES

Maximum age in years

150	120	50	30	20
Galápagos Tortoise	Box Turtle	American Alligator	Boa Constrictor	Komodo Dragon

Some Galápagos tortoises have been known to live to the old age of 150 years. Galápagos tortoises are also some of the largest tortoises in the world, weighing in at up to 500 pounds (226 kg). Even at their great size, these creatures can pull their heads, tails, and legs completely inside their shells. Amazingly, Galápagos tortoises can go without eating or drinking for many weeks. Approximately 10,000 of these tortoises live on the Galapagos island chain west of Ecuador.

World's
Largest Lizard

Komodo Dragon

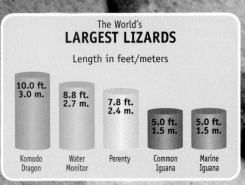

The World's
LARGEST LIZARDS

Length in feet/meters

Komodo Dragon	Water Monitor	Perenty	Common Iguana	Marine Iguana
10.0 ft. 3.0 m.	8.8 ft. 2.7 m.	7.8 ft. 2.4 m.	5.0 ft. 1.5 m.	5.0 ft. 1.5 m.

With a length of 10 feet (3 m) and a weight of 300 pounds (136 kg), Komodo dragons are the largest lizards roaming the Earth. A Komodo dragon has a long neck and tail, and strong legs. These members of the monitor family are found mainly on Komodo Island, located in the Lesser Sunda Islands of Indonesia. Komodos are dangerous and have even been known to attack and kill humans. A Komodo uses its sense of smell to locate food. It uses its long, yellow tongue to pick up an animal's scent. A Komodo can consume 80% of its body weight in just one meal!

World's Largest Reptile

Saltwater Crocodile

Saltwater crocodiles can grow to more than 22 feet (6.7 m) long. That's about twice the length of the average car. However, males usually measure only about 17 feet (5 m) long, and females normally reach about 10 feet (3 m) in length. A large adult will feed on buffalo, monkeys, cattle, wild boar, and other large mammals. Saltwater crocodiles are found throughout the East Indies and Australia. Despite their name, saltwater crocodiles can also be found in freshwater and swamps. Some other common names for this species are the estuary crocodile and the Indo-Pacific crocodile.

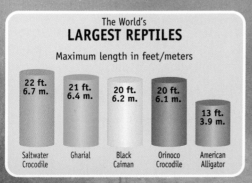

The World's
LARGEST REPTILES

Maximum length in feet/meters

22 ft. 6.7 m.	21 ft. 6.4 m.	20 ft. 6.2 m.	20 ft. 6.1 m.	13 ft. 3.9 m.
Saltwater Crocodile	Gharial	Black Caiman	Orinoco Crocodile	American Alligator

119

World's
Largest Spider

Goliath Birdeater

A Goliath birdeater is about the same size as a dinner plate—it can grow to a total length of 11 inches (28 cm) and weigh about 6 ounces (170 g). A Goliath's spiderlings are also big—they can have a 6-inch (15-cm) leg span after just one year. These giant tarantulas are found mostly in the rain forests of Guyana, Suriname, Brazil, and Venezuela. The Goliath birdeater's name is misleading—they commonly eat insects and small reptiles. Similar to other tarantula species, the Goliath birdeater lives in a burrow. The spider will wait by the opening to ambush prey that gets too close.

The World's
LARGEST SPIDERS

Length in inches/centimeters

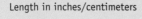

11 in. 28 cm.	10.5 in. 27 cm.	9 in. 23 cm.	8 in. 20 cm.	8 in. 20 cm.
Goliath Birdeater	Salmon Pink Birdeater	Slate Red Ornamental	King Baboon	Colombian Giant Redleg

World's
Fastest-Flying Insect

Hawk Moth

The average hawk moth—which got its name from its swift and steady flight—can cruise along at speeds of up to 33 miles (53 km) per hour. That's faster than the average speed limit on most city streets. Although they are found throughout the world, most species live in tropical climates. Also known as the sphinx moth and the hummingbird moth, this large insect can have a wingspan that reaches up to 8 inches (20 cm). The insect also has a good memory and may return to the same flowers at the same time each day.

The World's
FASTEST-FLYING INSECTS

Speed in miles/kilometers per hour

Hawk Moth	West Indian Butterfly	Deer Botfly	Dragonfly	Hornet
33.3 mph 53.6 kph	30.0 mph 48.2 kph	30.0 mph 48.2 kph	17.8 mph 28.6 kph	13.3 mph 21.4 kph

World's
Fastest-Running Insect

Australian Tiger Beetle

Australian tiger beetles can zip along at about 5.7 miles (9.2 km) per hour—that's about 170 body lengths per second! If a human could run at the same pace, he or she would run about 340 miles (547.2 km) per hour. Australian tiger beetles use their terrific speed to run down prey. Once a meal has been caught, the beetle chews it up in its powerful jaws and coats it in digestive juice. When the prey has become soft, the tiger beetle rolls it together and eats. These fierce beetles, which got their name from their skillful hunting, will also bite humans when provoked.

The World's
FASTEST-RUNNING INSECTS

Speed in miles/kilometers per hour

5.7 mph 9.2 kph	3.5 mph 5.6 kph	1.2 mph 1.9 kph	1.0 mph 1.6 kph	0.8 mph 1.3 kph
Australian Tiger Beetle	American Cockroach	Centipede	Ant	Mother-of-Pearl Caterpillar

World's Longest
Insect Migration

Monarch Butterfly

The World's
LONGEST INSECT MIGRATIONS

Migrations in miles/kilometers

2,700 mi. 4,345 km.	2,600 mi. 4,184 km.	2,500 mi. 4,023 km.	1,850 mi. 2,977 km.	300 mi. 483 km.
Monarch Butterfly	Desert Locust	Painted Lady Butterfly	Diamondback Moth	Ladybug

Millions of monarch butterflies travel to Mexico from all parts of North America every fall, flying up to 2,700 miles (4,345 km). Once there, they will huddle together in the trees and wait out the cold weather. In spring and summer, most butterflies only live four or five weeks as adults, but in the fall, a special generation of monarchs is born. These butterflies will live for about seven months and participate in the great migration to Mexico. Scientists are studying these butterflies in hope of learning how the insects know where and when to migrate to a place they—or several generations before them—have never visited.

World's Tallest Mountain

Mount Everest

Mount Everest's tallest peak towers 29,035 feet (8,850 m) into the air, and it is the highest point on Earth. This peak is an unbelievable 5.5 miles (8.8 km) above sea level. Mount Everest is located in the Himalayas, on the border between Nepal and Tibet. The mountain got its official name from surveyor Sir George Everest. In 1953, Sir Edmund Hillary and Tenzing Norgay were the first people to reach the peak. In 2008, the Olympic torch will be carried up to the top of the mountain on its way to the games in Beijing.

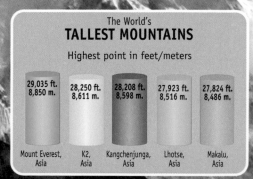

The World's
TALLEST MOUNTAINS

Highest point in feet/meters

29,035 ft. 8,850 m.	28,250 ft. 8,611 m.	28,208 ft. 8,598 m.	27,923 ft. 8,516 m.	27,824 ft. 8,486 m.
Mount Everest, Asia	K2, Asia	Kangchenjunga, Asia	Lhotse, Asia	Makalu, Asia

World's
Tallest Volcano

Ojos del Salado

The World's
TALLEST VOLCANOES
Height in feet/meters

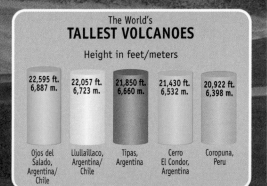

22,595 ft. 6,887 m.	22,057 ft. 6,723 m.	21,850 ft. 6,660 m.	21,430 ft. 6,532 m.	20,922 ft. 6,398 m.
Ojos del Salado, Argentina/ Chile	Llullaillaco, Argentina/ Chile	Tipas, Argentina	Cerro El Condor, Argentina	Coropuna, Peru

Located on the border of Argentina and Chile, Ojos del Salado towers 22,595 feet (6,887 m) above the surrounding Atacama Desert. It is the second-highest peak in the Andean mountain chain. Ojos del Salado is a composite volcano, which means that it is a tall, symmetrical cone that was built by layers of lava flow, ash, and cinder. There is no record of the volcano erupting, but this could be because of the volcano's remote location. Ojos del Salado is a very popular spot for mountain climbing.

World's Largest Lake

Caspian Sea

This giant inland body of saltwater stretches for almost 750 miles (1,207 km) from north to south, with an average width of about 200 miles (322 km). All together, it covers an area that's almost the same size as the state of California. The Caspian Sea is located east of the Caucasus Mountains in Central Asia. It is bordered by Iran, Russia, Kazakhstan, Azerbaijan, and Turkmenistan. The Caspian Sea has an average depth of about 550 feet (170 m). It is an important fishing resource, with species including sturgeon, salmon, perch, herring, and carp. Other animals live in the Caspian Sea, including porpoises, seals, and tortoises. The sea is estimated to be 30 million years old and became landlocked 5.5 million years ago.

The World's
LARGEST LAKES

Approximate area in
square miles/square kilometers

Caspian Sea, Asia	Superior, N. America	Victoria, Africa	Huron, N. America	Michigan, N. America
143,205 sq. mi. 370,901 sq. km.	31,820 sq. mi. 82,413 sq. km.	26,570 sq. mi. 68,816 sq. km.	23,010 sq. mi. 59,596 sq. km.	22,400 sq. mi. 58,016 sq. km.

World's Largest Desert

The Sahara

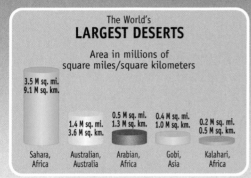

The World's
LARGEST DESERTS

Area in millions of
square miles/square kilometers

3.5 M sq. mi. 9.1 M sq. km.	1.4 M sq. mi. 3.6 M sq. km.	0.5 M sq. mi. 1.3 M sq. km.	0.4 M sq. mi. 1.0 M sq. km.	0.2 M sq. mi. 0.5 M sq. km.
Sahara, Africa	Australian, Australia	Arabian, Africa	Gobi, Asia	Kalahari, Africa

Located in northern Africa, the Sahara Desert covers approximately 3.5 million square miles (9.1 million sq km). It stretches for 5,200 miles (8,372 km) through the countries of Morocco, Algeria, Tunisia, Libya, Egypt, Mauritania, Mali, Niger, Chad, and Sudan. The Sahara gets very little rainfall—less than 8 inches (20 cm) per year. Even with its harsh environment, some 2.5 million people—mostly nomads—call the Sahara home. Date palms and acacias grow near oases. Some of the animals that live in the Sahara include gazelles, antelopes, jackals, foxes, and badgers.

World's Longest River

The Nile River in Africa stretches 4,145 miles (6,671 km), from the tributaries of Lake Victoria in Tanzania and Uganda out to the Mediterranean Sea. Because of varying depths, boats can sail on only about 2,000 miles (3,217 km) of the river. The Nile flows through Rwanda, Uganda, Sudan, and Egypt. The river's water supply is crucial to the existence of these African countries. The Nile's precious water is used to irrigate crops and to generate electricity. The Aswan Dam and the Aswan High Dam—both located in Egypt—are used to store the autumn floodwater for later use. The Nile is also used to transport goods from city to city along the river.

The Nile

The World's LONGEST RIVERS

Total length in miles/kilometers

4,145 mi. 6,671 km.	4,000 mi. 6,437 km.	3,740 mi. 6,021 km.	3,720 mi. 5,987 km.	3,650 mi. 5,877 km.
Nile, Africa	Amazon, S. America	Mississippi- Missouri, N. America	Yangtze, Asia	Yenisei, Angara, Asia

World's Greatest-Flowing River

Amazon

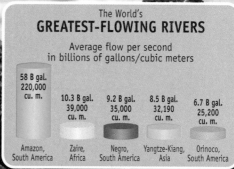

The World's
GREATEST-FLOWING RIVERS
Average flow per second
in billions of gallons/cubic meters

58 B gal. 220,000 cu. m.	10.3 B gal. 39,000 cu. m.	9.2 B gal. 35,000 cu. m.	8.5 B gal. 32,190 cu. m.	6.7 B gal. 25,200 cu. m.
Amazon, South America	Zaire, Africa	Negro, South America	Yangtze-Kiang, Asia	Orinoco, South America

The Amazon River moves more water than any other river in the world. It empties 58 billion gallons (220,000 cu m) per second into the Atlantic Ocean. At 4,080 miles (6,566 km), the Amazon is the second-longest river in the world. It contains more water than the Nile, Mississippi, and Yangtze rivers combined, and makes up more than 20% of the Earth's fresh water. The Amazon is also the world's widest river, measuring up to 7 miles (11 km) from bank to bank. The mouth of the Amazon measures about 200 miles (322 km), and contains the Marajo—the world's largest freshwater island.

World's Largest Ocean

Pacific

The Pacific Ocean covers almost 64 million square miles (166 million sq km) and reaches 36,200 feet (11,000 m) below sea level at its greatest depth—the Mariana Trench (near the Philippines). In fact, this ocean is so large that it covers about one-third of the planet (more than all of Earth's land put together) and holds more than half of all the seawater on Earth. The United States could fit inside this ocean 18 times! Some of the major bodies of water included in the Pacific are the Bering Sea, the Coral Sea, the Philippine Sea, and the Gulf of Alaska.

The World's
LARGEST OCEANS

Maximum area in millions of
square miles/square kilometers

64.0 M sq. mi.
165.7 M sq. km.

31.8 M sq. mi.
82.4 M sq. km.

25.3 M sq. mi.
65.5 M sq. km.

5.4 M sq. mi.
14.0 M sq. km.

| Pacific Ocean | Atlantic Ocean | Indian Ocean | Arctic Ocean |

World's Longest
Mountain Chain

The Andes

For 5,000 miles (8,050 km) the Andes extend through seven countries of South America—Venezuela, Colombia, Ecuador, Peru, Bolivia, Chile, and Argentina. The Andes also have some of the highest peaks in the world, with more than fifty of them measuring above 20,000 feet (6,100 m). Some of the animals found in the Andes include wild horses, vicuñas—members of the camel family, and chinchillas, furry members of the rodent family. The condor—the world's largest bird of prey—also calls these mountains its home.

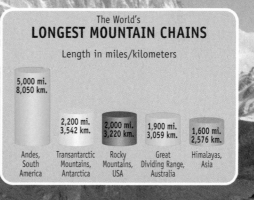

The World's
LONGEST MOUNTAIN CHAINS

Length in miles/kilometers

5,000 mi. 8,050 km.	2,200 mi. 3,542 km.	2,000 mi. 3,220 km.	1,900 mi. 3,059 km.	1,600 mi. 2,576 km.
Andes, South America	Transantarctic Mountains, Antarctica	Rocky Mountains, USA	Great Dividing Range, Australia	Himalayas, Asia

World's Largest Island

Greenland

Located in the North Atlantic Ocean, Greenland covers more than 840,000 square miles (2,175,600 sq km). Not including continents, it is the largest island in the world. Its jagged coastline is approximately 24,400 miles (39,267 km) long—about the same distance as Earth's circumference at the equator. Mountain chains are located on Greenland's east and west coasts, and the coastline is indented by fjords, or thin bodies of water bordered by steep cliffs. From north to south, the island stretches for about 1,660 miles (2,670 km). About 700,000 square miles (1,813,000 sq km) of this massive island are covered by a giant ice sheet. The island also contains the world's largest national park—Northeast Greenland National Park—with an area of 375,291 square miles (972,000 sq km).

The World's LARGEST ISLANDS

Approximate area in square miles/square kilometers

Greenland	New Guinea	Borneo	Madagascar	Baffin Island
840,070 sq. mi. 2,175,600 sq. km.	312,190 sq. mi. 808,572 sq. km.	289,961 sq. mi. 751,000 sq. km.	226,674 sq. mi. 587,086 sq. km.	195,926 sq. mi. 507,448 sq. km.

Country with the Most
Tropical Rain Forests

Brazil

The Countries with the
MOST TROPICAL RAIN FORESTS

Area in square miles/square kilometers

1,163,222 sq. mi. 3,012,731 sq. km.	521,512 sq. mi. 1,350,710 sq. km.	343,029 sq. mi. 888,441 sq. km.	292,032 sq. mi. 756,359 sq. km.	265,010 sq. mi. 686,373 sq. km.
Brazil, South America	Democratic Republic of Congo, Africa	Indonesia, Asia	Peru, South America	Bolivia, South America

Brazil—a large, tropical country in South America—has more than 1.16 million square miles (3.01 million sq km) of rain forest. The tropical forests of the Amazon River are located in the northern and north-central areas of the country. Amazonia, the world's largest rain forest, spreads across half of Brazil. The rain forest is home to 2.5 million insects, 500 mammals, 300 other reptile species, and a third of the world's birds. The rain forest is threatened, however, by timber companies, the growing human population, and ranchers clearing land for their herds to graze.

Country with the
Longest Coastline

Canada

The Countries with the
LONGEST COASTLINES

Total coastline in miles/kilometers

125,566 mi. 202,079 km.	33,999 mi. 54,717 km.	23,396 mi. 37,652 km.	22,559 mi. 36,305 km.	18,486 mi. 29,750 km.
Canada	Indonesia	Russia	Philippines	Japan

Canada's coastline measures 125,566 miles (202,079 km) long. If someone walked 12.5 miles (20.1 km) a day, it would take him or her about 33 years to walk its length. This measurement includes the mainland coast, as well as the coasts of the offshore islands. Of all the provinces and territories, Nunavut has the most coastline with 70,777 miles (113,904 km). The Canadian coast is made up of sandy beaches, towering cliffs, mudflats, marshes, and rocky piles. It also touches three oceans: the Pacific, the Atlantic, and the Arctic.

World's
Largest Diamond

Golden Jubilee

The World's
LARGEST DIAMONDS
Weight in carats

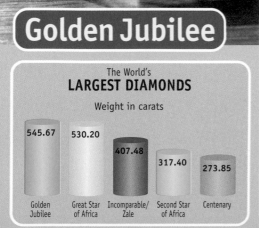

545.67	530.20	407.48	317.40	273.85
Golden Jubilee	Great Star of Africa	Incomparable/ Zale	Second Star of Africa	Centenary

The Golden Jubilee is the world's largest faceted diamond with a weight of 545.67 carats. This gigantic gem got its name when it was presented to the king of Thailand in 1997 for the Golden Jubilee— or 50th anniversary celebration—of his reign. The diamond was discovered in a South African mine in 1986 weighing 755.5 carats. Once it was cut, the diamond featured 148 perfectly symmetrical facets. The process took almost a year because of the diamond's size and multiple tension points. The diamond is on display at the Royal Museum of Bangkok in Thailand.

135

World's
Largest Fruit Crop

Tomatoes

More than 110 million tons (100.2 million t) of tomatoes are produced throughout the world each year. The world's top producers include the United States, Spain, Italy, Turkey, and China. Within the United States, about 180 square miles (466.2 sq km) are dedicated to growing the juicy, red fruit. California alone produces almost 10 million tons (9.1 M t). There is occasionally some confusion about whether the tomato is a fruit or vegetable. This is usually because cooks use the tomato as a vegetable, but scientists classify it as a fruit.

The World's
LARGEST FRUIT CROPS

Production in
millions of tons/metric tons

Tomatoes	Watermelons	Bananas	Oranges	Grapes
110.5 M tn / 100.2 M t	83.2 M tn / 75.5 M t	68.3 M tn / 62.0 M t	62.2 M tn / 56.4 M t	62.2 M tn / 56.4 M t

World's
Largest Vegetable Crop

Sugar Cane

The World's
LARGEST VEGETABLE CROPS

Production in billions
of tons/metric tons

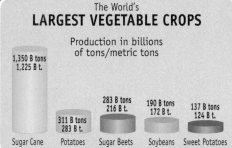

1,350 B tons
1,225 B t.
Sugar Cane

311 B tons
283 B t.
Potatoes

283 B tons
216 B t.
Sugar Beets

190 B tons
172 B t.
Soybeans

137 B tons
124 B t.
Sweet Potatoes

More than 1.35 billion tons (1.23 B t) of sugar cane is produced worldwide each year. Sugar cane is a type of tropical grass which resembles bamboo. The stalk takes about a year to mature, and can grow to 16.5 feet (5 m) high. The stalks are shredded and crushed to extract the juice, which is then heated and cooled to form sugar crystals. Sugar cane is used to produce about 70% of the world's sugar. About 105 countries grow the crop, and the top producers are Brazil and India.

Country That Eats the
Most Vegetables

Greece

The people of Greece eat almost 600 pounds (272 kg) of vegetables each year. Some of the most popular vegetables in Greek cuisine include eggplants, okra, zucchini, potatoes, and green beans. Approximately four-fifths of Greece is mountainous, which makes farming difficult. Only about 3% of the cultivated areas can be used for vegetable crops. Most of the country's vegetables are grown in the plains of Thessaly, Macedonia, and Thrace.

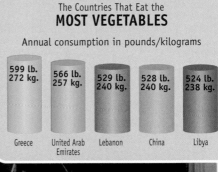

The Countries That Eat the
MOST VEGETABLES
Annual consumption in pounds/kilograms

Greece	United Arab Emirates	Lebanon	China	Libya
599 lb. 272 kg.	566 lb. 257 kg.	529 lb. 240 kg.	528 lb. 240 kg.	524 lb. 238 kg.

Country That Eats the Most Potato Chips

United Kingdom

People in the United Kingdom eat a lot of chips—averaging about 6.7 pounds (3.0 kg) per capita each year. This means that each person snacks on almost 14 bags in just 12 months, and some 8,500 million packages are sold each year! Better known as "crisps" in the United Kingdom, potato chips were first served in 1853 at a lodge in Saratoga Springs, New York. It takes about 10,000 pounds (4,536 kg) of potatoes to make 3,500 pounds (1,588 kg) of chips.

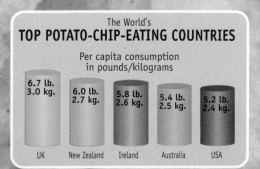

The World's
TOP POTATO-CHIP-EATING COUNTRIES

Per capita consumption
in pounds/kilograms

6.7 lb. 3.0 kg.	6.0 lb. 2.7 kg.	5.8 lb. 2.6 kg.	5.4 lb. 2.5 kg.	5.2 lb. 2.4 kg.
UK	New Zealand	Ireland	Australia	USA

Country That Drinks the Most Bottled Water

Italy

Italians like their bottled water—each person in the country drinks almost 47 gallons (178 l) of it each year. That averages to about a bottle and a half each day. The total amount of bottled water consumed in Italy each year averages 2.7 billion gallons (10.2 B l). There are about 175 mineral water sources in the country, which supply 280 brands of Italian bottled water.

Some of the most popular brands include San Pellegrino, San Gimignano, Ferrarelle, Aqua Panna, Lurisia, and Fiuggi. There are 700 different brands of bottled water sold worldwide.

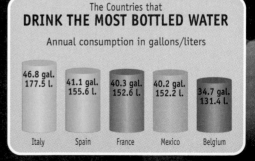

The Countries that
DRINK THE MOST BOTTLED WATER
Annual consumption in gallons/liters

Italy	Spain	France	Mexico	Belgium
46.8 gal. 177.5 l.	41.1 gal. 155.6 l.	40.3 gal. 152.6 l.	40.2 gal. 152.2 l.	34.7 gal. 131.4 l.

Country That Consumes the Most Soft Drinks

United States

Americans have an annual per capita soft drink consumption of 52.4 gallons (198.4 l). This means that each person in the country drinks an average of 559 cans of soda each year. Soda accounts for about 25% of all drinks consumed in the United States, and some 17.7 billion gallons (67.0 billion l) are sold annually. Recent studies show that diet sodas, as well as flavored sodas such as cherry, orange, and root beer, are becoming more popular than colas. The country's three top-selling soft drink companies are the Coca-Cola Company, PepsiCo Inc., and Dr Pepper/7UP.

The World's
TOP SODA-DRINKING COUNTRIES

Per capita consumption
in gallons/liters

USA	Mexico	Ireland	Norway	Canada
52.4 gal. 198.4 l.	36.1 gal. 136.7 l.	32.2 gal. 121.9 l.	31.4 gal. 118.9 l.	31.1 gal. 117.7 l.

Country That Eats the Most Chocolate

Switzerland

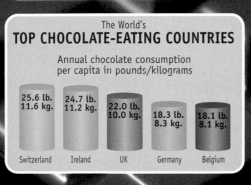

The World's
TOP CHOCOLATE-EATING COUNTRIES

Annual chocolate consumption per capita in pounds/kilograms

Switzerland	Ireland	UK	Germany	Belgium
25.6 lb. 11.6 kg.	24.7 lb. 11.2 kg.	22.0 lb. 10.0 kg.	18.3 lb. 8.3 kg.	18.1 lb. 8.1 kg.

The per-capita chocolate consumption in Switzerland is 25.6 pounds (11.6 kg) per year. That means approximately 181 million pounds (82 million kg) of chocolate are eaten in this small country each year. The Swiss chocolate market totaled more than $894 million in 2005. Chocolate has always been a popular food around the world. In fact, each year, approximately 594,000 tons (538,758 t) of cocoa beans—an important ingredient in chocolate—are consumed worldwide. Chocolate is consumed mainly in the form of candy.

Country That Eats the Most Ice Cream

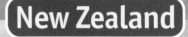

New Zealand

Each person in New Zealand eats an average of 55.6 pints (26.3 l) of ice cream every year. That's more than 1 pint per week. New Zealand also makes a lot of ice cream—about 15,000 tons (13,608 t) a year. The top flavors in New Zealand include vanilla, hokey pokey (vanilla with toffee bits), chocolate, and strawberry. Frozen treats were first served in the Roman Empire when people fixed fruit with ice. In the eighteenth century, ice cream became popular in France, England, and the United States. The ice-cream cone was first served in 1904 at the World's Fair in St. Louis, Missouri. Today, frozen dessert sales total billions of dollars worldwide.

The World's
TOP ICE-CREAM-EATING COUNTRIES

Per capita consumption in pints/liters

New Zealand	United States	Australia	Finland	Sweden
55.6 pt. 26.3 l.	39.5 pt. 18.7 l.	37.6 pt. 17.8 l.	29.4 pt. 13.9 l.	25.1 pt. 11.9 l.

143

Country That Eats the Most Meat

United States

Each person in the United States will eat about 264 pounds (119 kg) of meat this year. That's the same weight as 73 phone books. Beef is the most commonly eaten meat in the United States. Each American eats about 66 pounds (29.9 kg) of beef per year. In fact, an average 45 million pounds (20.4 million kg) of beef are eaten in the United States each day. The most common way to eat beef is in the form of a hamburger or cheeseburger. More than 85% of U.S. citizens ate one of these fast food items last year. Chicken is the second most popular meat, with each American eating about 60 pounds (27.2 kg) per year.

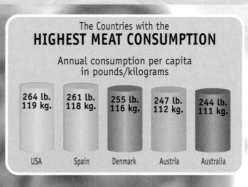

The Countries with the
HIGHEST MEAT CONSUMPTION

Annual consumption per capita
in pounds/kilograms

USA	Spain	Denmark	Austria	Australia
264 lb. 119 kg.	261 lb. 118 kg.	255 lb. 116 kg.	247 lb. 112 kg.	244 lb. 111 kg.

United States'
Greatest Snowfall

Mount Rainier

Mount Rainier had a record snowfall of 1,224 inches (3,109 cm) between 1971 and 1972. That's enough snow to cover a 10-story building! Located in the Cascade Mountains of Washington state, Mount Rainier is actually a volcano buried under 35 square miles (90.7 sq km) of snow and ice. The mountain, which covers about 100 square miles (259 sq km), reaches a height of 14,410 feet (4,392 m). Its three peaks include Liberty Cap, Point Success, and Columbia Crest. Mt. Rainier National Park was established in 1899.

The United States'
GREATEST ANNUAL SNOWFALLS

Highest annual snowfall
in inches/centimeters

1,224 in. 3,109 cm.	1,140 in. 2,895 cm.	1,122 in. 2,849 cm.	974 in. 2,474 cm.	964 in. 2,449 cm.
Mount Rainier, Washington, 1971–1972	Mount Baker, Washington, 1998–1999	Paradise Station, Washington, 1971–1972	Thompson Pass, Alaska, 1952–1953	Mount Copeland, British Columbia 1971–1972

World's Coldest
Inhabited Place

Resolute

The residents of Resolute, Canada have to bundle up—the average annual temperature is just -11.6° Fahrenheit (-22.8° C). Located on the northeast shore of Resolute Bay on the south coast of Cornwallis Island, the community is commonly the starting point for expeditions to the North Pole. In the winter it can stay dark for 24 hours, and in the summer it can stay light during the entire night. Only about 200 people brave the climate year-round, but the area is becoming quite popular with tourists.

146

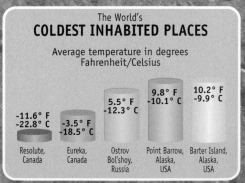

The World's
COLDEST INHABITED PLACES

Average temperature in degrees
Fahrenheit/Celsius

			9.8° F	10.2° F
		5.5° F	-10.1° C	-9.9° C
		-12.3° C		
-11.6° F				
-22.8° C	-3.5° F			
	-18.5° C			
Resolute,	Eureka,	Ostrov	Point Barrow,	Barter Island,
Canada	Canada	Bol'shoy,	Alaska,	Alaska,
		Russia	USA	USA

World's Hottest
Inhabited Place

The World's
HOTTEST INHABITED PLACES

Average temperature in degrees
Fahrenheit/Celsius

94.3° F 34.6° C	90.9° F 32.7° C	89.1° F 31.7° C	87.4° F 30.7° C	86.8° F 30.4° C
Dallol, Ethiopia	Bangkok, Thailand	Manila, Philippines	Singapore, Singapore	Assab, Eritrea

Throughout the year, temperatures in Dallol, Ethiopia, in Africa average 94.3° Fahrenheit (34.6° C). On some days it can reach 145° Fahrenheit (62.8° C) in the sun. Dallol is at the northernmost tip of the Great Rift Valley. The Dallol Depression reaches 328 feet (100 m) below sea level, making it the lowest point below sea level that is not covered by water. The area also has several active volcanoes. The only people to inhabit the region are the Afar, who have adapted to the harsh conditions there. For instance, to collect water the women build covered stone piles and wait for condensation to form on the rocks.

World's Wettest Inhabited Place

Cherrapunji

Each year, some 498 inches (1,265 cm) of rain falls on Cherrapunji, India. That's enough rain to cover a four-story building! Most of the region's rain falls within a six-month period, during the monsoon season. It's not uncommon for constant rain to pelt the area for two months straight without even a 10-minute break. During the other six months, the winds change and carry the rain away from Cherrapunji, leaving the ground dry and dusty. Ironically, this causes a drought throughout most of the area.

The World's WETTEST INHABITED PLACES

Average annual rainfall
in inches/centimeters

Cherrapunji, India	Mawsynram, India	Waialeale, Hawaii	Debundscha, Cameroon	Quibdo, Colombia
498 in. 1,265 cm.	467 in. 1,187 cm.	451 in. 1,146 cm.	404 in. 1,026 cm.	353 in. 897 cm.

World's Driest
Inhabited Place

Aswan

Each year, only .02 inches (.5 mm) of rain falls on Aswan, Egypt. In the country's sunniest and southernmost city, summer temperatures can reach a blistering 114° Fahrenheit (46° C). Aswan is located on the west bank of the Nile River. The Aswan High Dam, at 12,565 feet (3,830 m) long, is the city's most famous landmark. It produces the majority of Egypt's power in the form of hydroelectricity. Aswan also has many Pharaonic, Greco-Roman, and Muslim ruins.

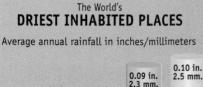

The World's
DRIEST INHABITED PLACES

Average annual rainfall in inches/millimeters

0.02 in. 0.50 mm.	0.03 in. 0.76 mm.	0.03 in. 0.76 mm.	0.09 in. 2.3 mm.	0.10 in. 2.5 mm.
Aswan, Egypt	Arica, Chile	Luxor, Egypt	Ica, Peru	Wadi Halfa, Sudan

Place with the World's
Fastest Winds

Mount Washington

The World's
FASTEST WINDS

Speed of strongest winds
in miles/kilometers per hour

**231 mph
372 kph** — Mount Washington, New Hampshire, USA

**200 mph
322 kph** — Commonwealth Bay, Antarctica

**185 mph
298 kph** — South Pole, Antarctica

**125 mph
201 kph** — New Orleans, Louisiana, USA

**94 mph
151 kph** — Valdez, Alaska, USA

The wind gusts at the top of Mount Washington reached 231 miles (372 km) per hour in 1934—and these gusts were not part of a storm. Normally, the average wind speed at the summit of this mountain is approximately 36 miles (58 km) per hour. Located in the White Mountains of New Hampshire, Mount Washington is the highest peak in New England at 6,288 feet (1,917 m). The treeless summit, which is known for its harsh weather, has an average annual temperature of only 26.5° Fahrenheit (-3.1° C).

World's
Tallest Weed

Giant Hogweed

Growing to a height of 12 feet (3.6 m), the giant hogweed can have leaves that measure 3 feet (91 cm) long. This weed is taller than some trees! The giant hogweed is part of the parsley, or carrot, family and it has hollow stalks with tiny white flowers. Although it was first brought to America from Asia as an ornamental plant, the hogweed quickly became a pest. Each plant can produce about 50,000 seeds and the weed quickly spreads through its environment.

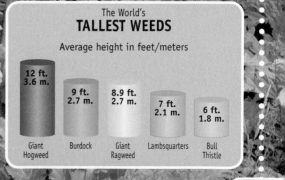

The World's
TALLEST WEEDS

Average height in feet/meters

Giant Hogweed	Burdock	Giant Ragweed	Lambsquarters	Bull Thistle
12 ft. 3.6 m.	9 ft. 2.7 m.	8.9 ft. 2.7 m.	7 ft. 2.1 m.	6 ft. 1.8 m.

World's Largest Leaves

Raffia Palm

The raffia palm tree has leaves that reach lengths of 65 feet (19.8 m) long—about the same length as a regulation tennis court. Raffia trees have several stems that can reach heights of 6 to 30 feet (2 to 9 m). When they reach about 50 years of age, raffia palms flower and produce egg-size fruits covered in hard scales. Several products come from these palms, including raffia, and floor and shoe polish. Raffia leaves are also used to weave baskets, mats, and hats. These enormous plants are native to Madagascar, but most of the native growth has been overharvested. The palms are now cultivated in West and East Africa.

The World's
LARGEST LEAVES

Length in feet/meters

65 ft. 19.8 m.			16 ft. 5 m.	13 ft. 4 m.
	20 ft. 6 m.	18 ft. 5.5 m.		
Raffia Palm	Fan Palm	Date Palm	Coconut Palm	Oil Palm

World's Tallest Cactus

Saguaro

Many saguaro cacti grow to a height of 50 feet (15 m), but some have actually reached 75 feet (23 m). That's taller than a seven-story building. Saguaros start out quite small and grow very slowly. A saguaro only reaches about 1 inch (2.5 cm) high during its first 10 years. It will not bloom until it is between 50 and 75 years old. By this time, the cactus has a strong root system that can support about 9 to 10 tons (8 to 9 t) of growth. Its spines can measure up to 2.5 inches (5 cm) long. Saguaro cacti live for about 170 years. The giant cactus can be found from southeastern California to southern Arizona.

The World's
TALLEST CACTI

Height in feet/meters

50–75 ft. 15–23 m.	40–50 ft. 12–15 m.	33 ft. 10 m.	30 ft. 9 m.	12 ft. 3.7 m.
Saguaro	Organ Pipe	Opuntia	Cane Cholla	Barrel

Country That Produces the Most Fruit

China

Each year, China produces about 74 million tons (67 M t) of fruit—about 14% of the world's total fruit production. The country's fruit crop is worth about $13 billion annually. China is the world's top producer of apples and pears, and ranks third in the world for citrus fruit production. The country's orchards total about 21.5 million acres (8.6 M ha)—almost a quarter of the world's orchard land. More than half of China's population works in the agriculture industry.

The Countries that Produce the
MOST FRUIT

Millions of tons/metric tons
produced annually

China	India	Brazil	USA	Mexico
74.3 M tons 67.1 M t.	46.1 M tons 41.8 M t.	35.7 M tons 32.4 M t.	32.2 M tons 29.2 M t.	17.4 M tons 15.8 M t.

World's Tallest Tree

California Redwood

Growing in both California and southern Oregon, California redwoods can reach a height of 385 feet (117.4 m). Their trunks can grow up to 25 feet (7.6 m) in diameter. The tallest redwood on record stands 385 feet (117.4 m) tall—more than 60 feet (18.3 m) taller than the Statue of Liberty. Amazingly, this giant tree grows from a seed the size of a tomato. Some redwoods are believed to be more than 2,000 years old. The trees' thick bark and foliage protect them from natural hazards such as insects and fires.

The World's TALLEST TREE SPECIES

Height in feet/meters

California Redwood	Giant Sequoia	Eucalyptus	Douglas Fir	Japanese Cedar
100–385 ft. 30–117 m.	150–325 ft. 46–99 m.	250–300 ft. 76–91 m.	200–250 ft. 61–63 m.	150–175 ft. 46–53 m.

World's Most
Poisonous Mushroom

Death Cap

The World's
MOST POISONOUS MUSHROOMS

Ranked 1–5 by likeliness to
cause death in humans

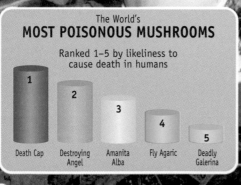

1	2	3	4	5
Death Cap	Destroying Angel	Amanita Alba	Fly Agaric	Deadly Galerina

Death cap mushrooms are members of the Amanita family, which are among the most dangerous mushrooms in the world. The death cap contains deadly peptide toxins that cause rapid loss of bodily fluids and intense thirst. Within six hours, the poison shuts down the kidneys, liver, and central nervous system, causing coma and—in more than 50% of cases—death. Estimates of the number of poisonous mushroom species range from 80 to 2,000. Most experts agree, however, that at least 100 varieties will cause severe symptoms and even death if eaten.

World's Largest Flower

Rafflesia

The World's LARGEST FLOWERS

Maximum flower size in inches/centimeters

36 in. 91 cm.	19 in. 48 cm.	18 in. 46 cm.	14 in. 36 cm.	10 in. 25 cm.
Rafflesia	Sunflower	Giant Water Lily	Brazilian Dutchman	Magnolia

The blossoms of the giant rafflesia—or "stinking corpse lily"—can reach 36 inches (91 cm) in diameter and weigh up to 25 pounds (11 kg). Its petals can grow 1.5 feet (0.5 m) long and 1 inch (2.5 cm) thick. There are 16 different species of Rafflesia. This endangered plant is found only in the rain forests of Borneo and Sumatra. It lives inside the bark of host vines and is noticeable only when its flowers break through to blossom. The large, reddish-purple flowers give off a smell similar to rotting meat, which attracts insects to help spread the rafflesia's pollen.

World's
Deadliest Plant

Castor Bean Plant

The World's
DEADLIEST PLANTS
Risk of fatality if consumed

Extreme	High	High		
			Medium	
				Low
Castor Bean	Rosary Bead	Foxglove	Azalea	English Ivy

The castor bean plant produces seeds that contain a protein called ricin. Scientists estimate that ricin is about 6,000 times more poisonous than cyanide and 12,000 times more poisonous than rattlesnake venom. It would take a particle of ricin only about the size of a grain of sand to kill a 160-pound (73 kg) adult. The deadly beans are actually quite pretty and are sometimes used in jewelry. Castor bean plants grow in warmer climates and can reach a height of about 10 feet (3 m). Its leaves can measure up to 2 feet (0.6 m) wide.

World's Largest Seed

Coco de Mer

Some of the World's
LARGEST SEEDS

Length in inches/centimeters

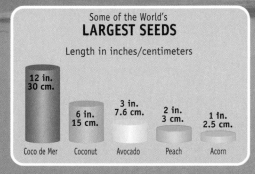

12 in. 30 cm.				
	6 in. 15 cm.	3 in. 7.6 cm.	2 in. 3 cm.	1 in. 2.5 cm.
Coco de Mer	Coconut	Avocado	Peach	Acorn

Measuring 3 feet (1 m) in diameter and 12 inches (30 cm) in length, the giant, dark-brown seed of the coco de mer palm tree can weigh up to 40 pounds (18 kg). Only a few thousand seeds are produced each year. Coco de mer trees are found on the island of Praslin in the Seychelles Archipelago of the Indian Ocean. The area where some of the few remaining trees grow has been declared a Natural World Heritage Site in an effort to protect the species from poachers looking for the rare seeds. The tree can grow up to 100 feet (31 m) tall, with leaves measuring 20 feet (6 m) long and 12 feet (3.6 m) wide.

World's Highest
Tsunami Wave Since 1900

Lituya Bay

A 1,720-foot- (524 m) high tsunami wave crashed down in Lituya Bay, Alaska, on July 9, 1958. Located in Glacier Bay National Park, the tsunami was caused by a massive landslide that was triggered by an 8.3 magnitude earthquake. The water from the bay covered 5 square miles (13 sq km) of land and traveled inland as far as 3,600 feet (1,097 m). Millions of trees were washed away. Amazingly, because the area was very isolated and the coastline was sheltered by coves, only two people died when their fishing boat sank.

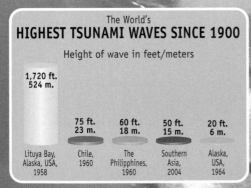

The World's
HIGHEST TSUNAMI WAVES SINCE 1900

Height of wave in feet/meters

1,720 ft. 524 m.	75 ft. 23 m.	60 ft. 18 m.	50 ft. 15 m.	20 ft. 6 m.
Lituya Bay, Alaska, USA, 1958	Chile, 1960	The Philipphines, 1960	Southern Asia, 2004	Alaska, USA, 1964

World's Most Intense
Earthquake Since 1900

Coastal Chile

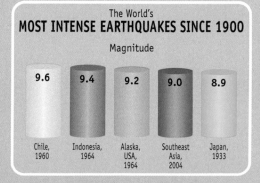

The World's
MOST INTENSE EARTHQUAKES SINCE 1900

Magnitude

9.6	9.4	9.2	9.0	8.9
Chile, 1960	Indonesia, 1964	Alaska, USA, 1964	Southeast Asia, 2004	Japan, 1933

An explosive earthquake measuring 9.5 on the Richter scale rocked the coast of Chile on May 22, 1960. This is equal to the intensity of about 60,000 hydrogen bombs. Some 2,000 people were killed and another 3,000 injured. The death toll was fairly low because the foreshocks frightened people into the streets. When the massive jolt came, many of the collapsed buildings were already empty. The coastal towns of Valdivia and Puerto Montt suffered the most damage because they were closest to the epicenter—located about 100 miles (161 km) offshore.

World's Most Destructive
Flood Since 1900

Hurricane Katrina

The pounding rain and storm surges of Hurricane Katrina resulted in catastrophic flooding that cost about $60 billion. The storm formed in late August 2005 over the Bahamas, moved across Florida, and finally hit Louisiana on August 29 as a category 3 storm. The storm surge from the Gulf of Mexico flooded the state, as well as neighboring Alabama and Mississippi. Many levees could not hold back the massive amounts of water, and entire towns were destroyed. In total, some 1,800 people lost their lives.

The World's
MOST DESTRUCTIVE FLOODS SINCE 1900

Cost of damages, in billions of US dollars

$60.0B	$30.0B	$27.0B	$24.0B	$18.0B
Hurricane Katrina, USA, 2005	Yangtze River, China, 1998	Bangladesh, 1970	Yangtze River, China, 1990	Great Midwest Flood, USA, 1993

World's
Worst Oil Spill

On March 16, 1978, the *Amoco Cadiz* hit ground in shallow water off the coast of Brittany, France and spilled 220,000 tons (199,581 t) of oil into the English Channel. The very large crude carrier encountered strong storms and lost the ability to steer. Tug boats and the ship's anchor were unable to stop the tanker from drifting, and it collided with the rocky shore. The ship's hull and storage tanks were ripped open, and 68.7 million gallons (260 million l) of oil spread across 125 miles (201 km) of the Brittany coastline. The oil slick ruined fisheries, oyster beds, and surrounding beaches.

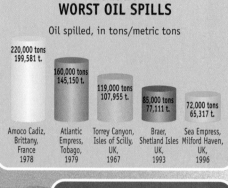

The World's
WORST OIL SPILLS

Oil spilled, in tons/metric tons

220,000 tons 199,581 t.	160,000 tons 145,150 t.	119,000 tons 107,955 t.	85,000 tons 77,111 t.	72,000 tons 65,317 t.
Amoco Cadiz, Brittany, France 1978	Atlantic Empress, Tobago, 1979	Torrey Canyon, Isles of Scilly, UK, 1967	Braer, Shetland Isles UK, 1993	Sea Empress, Milford Haven, UK, 1996

Amoco Cadiz

World's Most Destructive
Tornado Since 1900

Oklahoma City

On May 3, 1999, a devastating tornado swept through downtown Oklahoma City, Oklahoma, killing 36 people and causing more than $1.2 billion in damages. This powerful twister traveled almost 38 miles (61 km) in four hours and measured a mile (1.6 km) wide at times. With raging winds reaching 318 miles (512 km) per hour, it was the strongest wind speed ever recorded. More than 800 houses were destroyed in Oklahoma City alone. Because of the mass destruction caused by this twister, it was classified as a five—the second-highest possible rating—on the Fujita Tornado Scale.

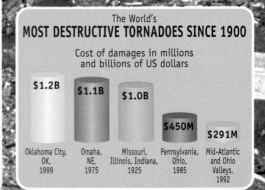

The World's
MOST DESTRUCTIVE TORNADOES SINCE 1900

Cost of damages in millions
and billions of US dollars

$1.2B	$1.1B	$1.0B	$450M	$291M
Oklahoma City, OK, 1999	Omaha, NE, 1975	Missouri, Illinois, Indiana, 1925	Pennsylvania, Ohio, 1985	Mid-Atlantic and Ohio Valleys, 1992

World's Most Intense Hurricane Since 1900

Hurricane Gilbert

The World's
MOST INTENSE HURRICANES SINCE 1900

Highest sustained wind speed
in miles/kilometers per hour

184 mph 296 kph	180 mph 290 kph	175 mph 282 kph	165 mph 266 kph	165 mph 266 kph
Hurricane Gilbert, 1988	Hurricane Mitch, 1998	Hurricane Katrina, 2005	Hurricane Allen, 1980	Hurricane Camille, 1969

During mid-September 1988, Hurricane Gilbert blew through the Atlantic, Caribbean, and Gulf of Mexico, destroying almost everything in its path. It devastated most of the island of Jamaica on September 10th, and later caused major flooding in the Yucatán Peninsula and in Northern Mexico five days later. Gilbert was classified as a category five hurricane—the most destructive hurricane rating on the Saffir-Simpson Hurricane Scale—for five days. The storm's top wind speeds reached 184 miles (296 km) per hour. The total clean-up cost for the hurricane was more than $5 billion. Some 318 people also lost their lives in the terrible storm.

Popular Culture
Records

**Television • Music • Theater
Movies • Books • Art**

Most Popular Television Show

CSI: Crime Scene Investigation

Most Popular TELEVISION SHOWS

Average audience percentage in 2005

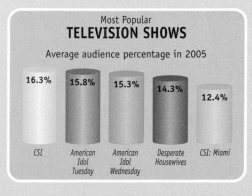

CSI	American Idol Tuesday	American Idol Wednesday	Desperate Housewives	CSI: Miami
16.3%	15.8%	15.3%	14.3%	12.4%

Averaging 16.3% of the television viewing audience each Thursday, *CSI: Crime Scene Investigation* is a smash hit for CBS. The hour-long drama features a team of forensic specialists who work for the Las Vegas Police Department's Crime Scene Investigation unit. Gil Grissom, played by William Petersen, leads the team of scientists, including Sara (Jorja Fox), Catherine (Marg Helgenberger), Warrick (Gary Dourdan), and Nick (George Eads). The show has been so popular, it has inspired two spin-offs—*CSI: Miami* and *CSI: New York*.

167

Highest-Paid TV Actor

James Gandolfini

For each episode of *The Sopranos* he filmed, James Gandolfini earned $1 million. Gandolfini played Tony Soprano, the head of a New Jersey mobster family in the popular crime drama on HBO. *The Sopranos* began in 1999 and ran until 2006. During that time, Gandolfini won an Emmy® Award, four SAG Awards, and three Golden Globe Awards. On the big screen, Gandolfini is also a big hit. Some of his movie credits include *Get Shorty* (1995), *Crimson Tide* (1995), *The Mexican* (2001), and *Surviving Christmas* (2004).

Highest-Paid
TV ACTORS

Money earned per episode during the 2005–2006 season, in US dollars

$1.0 M	$350,000	$175,000	$100,000	$90,400
James Gandolfini, *The Sopranos*	William Petersen, *CSI*	Gary Sinise, *CSI: New York*	Donald Trump, *The Apprentice*	Matthew Fox, *Lost*

Highest-Paid
TV Actress

Teri Hatcher

Teri Hatcher earns $295,870 per episode for her role as Susan Mayer on *Desperate Housewives*. Hatcher plays a single mom raising a teenage daughter on the now famous Wisteria Lane. Since the show began in 2004, Hatcher has won a Golden Globe Award for Best Actress, a 2005 Screen Actors Guild Award for Outstanding Performance by a Female Actor, and a 2005 Television Critics Award. Hatcher's other most well-known roles include Lois Lane in *Lois & Clark: The New Adventures of Superman*, and Paris Carver in the film *Tomorrow Never Dies*.

Highest-Paid
TV ACTRESSES

Money earned per episode during the
2005–2006 season, in US dollars

$295,870 $260,870 $260,870 $150,000 $150,000

| Teri Hatcher, *Desperate Housewives* | Marcia Cross, *Desperate Housewives* | Felicity Huffman, *Desperate Housewives* | Marg Helgenberger, *CSI* | Jorja Fox, *CSI* |

Highest-Paid
Talk Show Host

Oprah Winfrey pulled in $225 million in 2005, making her the world's top-paid entertainer. In total, she is worth more than $1.2 billion. Oprah's self-made millions have come mostly from her television show, which began in 1983. Since then, Oprah has been educating her viewers and helping her audience with tough social issues. The megastar is also involved in movies, television production, magazines, books, radio, and the Internet. Oprah is also known for her great generosity, and has donated millions to various charities.

Highest-Paid
TV TALK SHOW HOSTS
Income in 2005

$225 M	$40 M	$30 M	$28 M	$20 M
Oprah Winfrey	David Letterman	Jay Leno	Judge Judy Sheindlin	Regis Philbin

United States' Best-Selling
Male Recording Artist

Elvis Presley

Elvis Presley has sold more than 116.5 million records since he first signed with RCA Records back in 1955. Presley's unique sound and dance moves captured fans' attention around the world. Known as the King of Rock and Roll, Presley also holds the record for the solo singer with the most chart hits at 151. Some of his most famous songs include "Love Me Tender," "Blue Suede Shoes," "Jailhouse Rock," and "All Shook Up." Presley also had an impressive film career. He appeared in more than 30 films, which earned a combined total of about $150 million at the box office. Presley died in 1977.

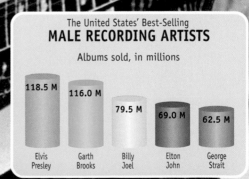

The United States' Best-Selling
MALE RECORDING ARTISTS

Albums sold, in millions

Elvis Presley	Garth Brooks	Billy Joel	Elton John	George Strait
118.5 M	116.0 M	79.5 M	69.0 M	62.5 M

United States' Best-Selling
Female Recording Artist

Barbra Streisand

Barbra Streisand has sold almost 71 million copies of her work during her 39 years as a singer. She has recorded more than 50 albums and has more gold albums—or albums that have sold at least 500,000 copies—than any other entertainer in history. Streisand has 47 gold albums, 28 platinum albums, and 13 multiplatinum albums. Some of her recordings include "I Finally Found Someone" (1996), "Tell Him" (1997), and "If You Ever Leave Me" (1999). Some of her best-known film work includes roles in *Funny Girl, The Way We Were, Yentl,* and *Meet the Fockers.* Streisand has won 10 Grammys®, 2 Academy Awards®, 6 Emmy® Awards, and 11 Golden Globes.

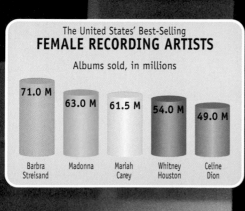

The United States' Best-Selling
FEMALE RECORDING ARTISTS

Albums sold, in millions

Barbra Streisand	Madonna	Mariah Carey	Whitney Houston	Celine Dion
71.0 M	63.0 M	61.5 M	54.0 M	49.0 M

World's Top-Earning
Male Singer

Paul McCartney

Paul McCartney earned $77.3 million in 2005. The former Beatle went on a 28-stop U.S. tour to promote his *Chaos and Creation in the Backyard*. McCartney also sang several favorite Beatles and Wings songs he hadn't performed in 15 years. In 2005, McCartney also entertained fans during the Super Bowl halftime show, and released a children's book. He has won 13 Grammy® Awards during his legendary career. McCartney was inducted into the Rock & Roll Hall of Fame in 1988 as a member of the Beatles, and later as a solo artist in 1999.

The World's Top-Earning
MALE SINGERS OF 2005

Income in
millions of US dollars

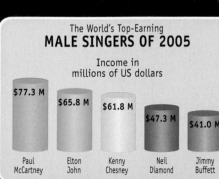

Paul McCartney	Elton John	Kenny Chesney	Neil Diamond	Jimmy Buffett
$77.3 M	$65.8 M	$61.8 M	$47.3 M	$41.0 M

World's Top-Earning
Female Singer

Celine Dion

During 2005, Celine Dion brought in $81.3 million. Her biggest moneymaking venture was her partnership with Caesars Palace in Las Vegas, Nevada. Her show, entitled A New Day, features Dion's songs in a theatrical production. Dion began the show in 2003, and will perform five nights a week for forty weeks a year for three years. The French-Canadian singer has sold more than 155 million albums worldwide. She has won Grammy® Awards in the United States, Juno and Felix Awards in Canada, and World Music Awards in Europe.

The World's Top-Earning
FEMALE SINGERS OF 2005

Income in millions
of US dollars

Celine Dion	Madonna	Shania Twain	Bette Midler	Gwen Stefani
$81.3 M	$50.0 M	$34.0 M	$31.0 M	$24.2 M

United States' Best-Selling
Recording Group

The Beatles

The Beatles have sold 168.5 million copies of their music since their first official recording session in September 1962. In the two years that followed, they had 26 Top 40 singles. John Lennon, Paul McCartney, George Harrison, and Ringo Starr made up the "Fab Four," as the Beatles were known. Together they recorded many albums that are now considered rock masterpieces, such as *Rubber Soul, Sgt. Pepper's Lonely Hearts Club Band,* and *The Beatles.* The group broke up in 1969. In 2001, however, their newly released greatest hits album—*The Beatles 1*—reached the top of the charts. One of their best-known songs— "Yesterday"—is the most recorded song in history, with about 2,500 different artists recording their own versions.

The United States'
BEST-SELLING RECORDING GROUP

Millions of albums sold

The Beatles	Led Zeppelin	The Eagles	Pink Floyd	AC/DC
168.5 M	109.5 M	91.0 M	73.5 M	66.0 M

Male Singer with the
Most Chart Hits

Elvis Presley

Elvis Presley is truly the King of Rock and Roll with an unprecedented 151 chart hits during his electrifying career. He also holds several other records, including the most Top 40 hits with 107, the most Top 10 hits with 38, the most consecutive number-one hits with 10, and the most weeks at number one with 80. Influenced by gospel, blues, and jazz, some of Presley's greatest hits include "Don't Be Cruel," "Hound Dog," "Heartbreak Hotel," and "Are You Lonesome Tonight?" And Elvis remains popular today—a greatest-hits album was released twenty-five years after his death and reached number one on the U.S. and U.K. charts.

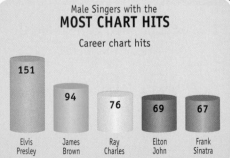

Male Singers with the
MOST CHART HITS

Career chart hits

Elvis Presley	James Brown	Ray Charles	Elton John	Frank Sinatra
151	94	76	69	67

Female Singer with the
Most Chart Hits

Aretha Franklin

Music legend Aretha Franklin has scored a record 76 chart hits during her career. Franklin began her career singing gospel music as a teenager in the 1950s. She quickly rose to fame in the 1960s, and she had 10 Top 10 hits between 1967 and 1968. During her more than 40 years as a singer, Franklin has recorded almost 50 albums. Some of her greatest hits include "Respect," "I Never Loved a Man," "I Say a Little Prayer," and "Bridge Over Troubled Water." The Queen of Soul became the first woman inducted into the Rock and Roll Hall of Fame in 1987.

Female Singers with the
MOST CHART HITS
Career chart hits

Aretha Franklin	Connie Francis	Dionne Warwick	Brenda Lee	Madonna
76	56	56	55	50

World's Top-Earning Band

The Rolling Stones

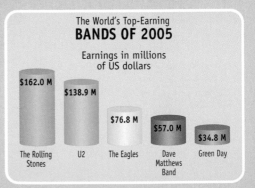

The Rolling Stones set a record for the highest-grossing concert of all time with ticket sales totaling $162 million. This is especially impressive because the Stones only played 42 shows. Tickets to see the legendary rock group average $134 apiece. The tour promoted the group's new album, *The Bigger Bang*—the Stones' first new album in eight years. Some of the new songs include "Streets of Love," "Rough Justice," and "Back of My Hand." In 2006, the Stones rocked the crowd during halftime at Super Bowl XL.

The World's Top-Earning
BANDS OF 2005

Earnings in millions
of US dollars

Band	Earnings
The Rolling Stones	$162.0 M
U2	$138.9 M
The Eagles	$76.8 M
Dave Matthews Band	$57.0 M
Green Day	$34.8 M

Singer with the Most
Country Music Awards

Vince Gill

Since his debut album *Turn Me Loose* in 1984, country superstar Vince Gill has won 18 Country Music Awards. He won his first Country Music Award in 1990 for Single of the Year with "When I Call Your Name." Since then, he has won Male Vocalist of the Year five times, Song of the Year four times, Vocal Event of the Year four times, Entertainer of the Year twice, and Album of the Year twice. Gill also hosted the Country Music Awards from 1992 to 2003. Some of Gill's most successful albums include *The Key* (1998), *Let's Make Sure We Kiss Goodbye* (2000), and *Next Big Thing* (2003).

Singers with the Most
COUNTRY MUSIC AWARDS
Number of awards

18	16	15	11	10
Vince Gill	Alan Jackson	Brooks & Dunn	Garth Brooks	Dixie Chicks

Play with the
Most Tony Awards

The Producers

In March 2001, *The Producers* took home 12 of its record-breaking 15 Tony® nominations. The Broadway smash won awards for Best Musical, Best Original Score, Best Book, Best Direction of a Musical, Best Choreography, Best Orchestration, Best Scenic Design, Best Costume Design, Best Lighting Design, Best Actor in a Musical, Best Featured Actor in a Musical, and Best Actress in a Musical. *The Producers,* which starred Nathan Lane and Matthew Broderick, is a stage adaptation of Mel Brooks's 1968 movie. Brooks wrote the lyrics and music for 16 new songs for the stage version.

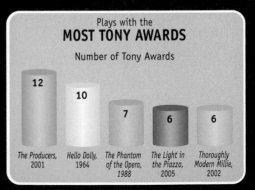

Plays with the
MOST TONY AWARDS

Number of Tony Awards

The Producers, 2001	Hello Dolly, 1964	The Phantom of the Opera, 1988	The Light in the Piazza, 2005	Thoroughly Modern Millie, 2002
12	10	7	6	6

World's Longest-Running Broadway Show

Phantom of the Opera

The Phantom of the Opera has been performed more than 7,581 times since the show opened in January 1988. The show tells the story of a disfigured musical genius who terrorizes the performers of the Paris Opera House. More than 80 million people have seen a performance, and box-office receipts total more than $3.2 billion. The show won seven Tony Awards its opening year, including Best Musical. The musical drama is performed at the Majestic Theatre.

The World's Longest-Running
BROADWAY SHOWS

Total performances*

7,581	7,485	6,680	6,137	5,959
The Phantom of the Opera, 1988–	Cats, 1982–2000	Les Misérables, 1987–2003	A Chorus Line, 1975–1990	Oh! Calcutta!, 1969–1972

*As of April 2, 2006

Actor with the Highest Career
Box-Office Earnings

Samuel L. Jackson

Samuel L. Jackson has appeared in more than 80 movies, and leads all other actors with box-office earnings, totaling more than $3.8 billion! Some of his most well-known movies include *Do The Right Thing* (1989), *Jurassic Park* (1993), *Pulp Fiction* (1994), *Die Hard with a Vengeance* (1995), and *Coach Carter* (2005). He also appeared in all three *Star Wars* prequel movies as Mace Windu. Jackson was honored with a star on the Hollywood Walk of Fame in 2000.

Actors with the Highest
CAREER BOX-OFFICE EARNINGS

Earnings in billions
of US dollars*

$3.81 B	$3.26 B	$3.10 B	$2.91 B	$2.91 B
Samuel L. Jackson	Harrison Ford	Tom Hanks	Tom Cruise	Eddie Murphy

*As of March 18, 2006

182

World's Top-Grossing
Kids' Movie

Snow White and the Seven Dwarfs

The World's
TOP-GROSSING KIDS' MOVIES

Box-office receipts in billions and
millions of dollars adjusted for inflation

$1.03 B	$977 M	$921 M	$890 M	$877 M
Snow White and the Seven Dwarfs, 1937	Harry Potter and the Sorcerer's Stone, 2001	Shrek 2, 2004	Harry Potter and the Goblet of Fire, 2005	Harry Potter and the Chamber of Secrets, 2002

Walt Disney's *Snow White and the Seven Dwarfs* has earned an amazing $1.03 billion in box-office receipts in the 69 years since its debut. (To compare the success of films throughout the decades, it is necessary to adjust for inflation.) More than 750 artists were used during the three-year production. *Snow White and the Seven Dwarfs* was the first-ever animated feature film, and it cost $1.4 million to make. Many of the songs in the movie, including "Some Day My Prince Will Come" and "Whistle While You Work," have become true American classics.

Most Successful Movie
Opening Weekend

Spider-Man

The comic-book thriller *Spider-Man* earned an amazing $114.8 million on the first weekend in May 2002. The box-office receipts from this one weekend made up more than a quarter of the film's total gross of $404 million. The Sony film—which opened in more than 3,600 movie theaters across the country—starred Tobey Maguire as Spider-Man and Kirsten Dunst as his love interest, Mary Jane Watson. Willem Dafoe played the movie's villain—the Green Goblin.

Movies with the
BEST OPENING WEEKENDS

Weekend earnings in millions of US dollars

$114.8 M	$108.4 M	$108.0 M	$102.7 M	$93.7 M
Spider-Man 5/3/02	Star Wars: Episode III— Revenge of the Sith 5/19/05	Shrek 2 5/19/04	Harry Potter and the Goblet of Fire 11/18/05	Harry Potter and the Prisoner of Azkaban 6/4/04

Movies with the Most Oscars®

Ben-Hur, The Lord of the Rings: The Return of the King, Titanic

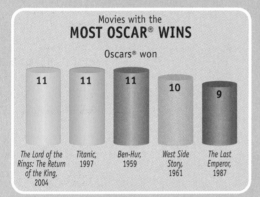

Movies with the MOST OSCAR® WINS

Oscars® won

11	11	11	10	9
The Lord of the Rings: The Return of the King, 2004	Titanic, 1997	Ben-Hur, 1959	West Side Story, 1961	The Last Emperor, 1987

Cast and crew members with some of the 11 Oscars® for *The Lord of the Rings: The Return of the King*

The only three films in Hollywood history to win 11 Academy Awards® are *Ben-Hur, The Lord of the Rings: The Return of the King,* and *Titanic.* Some of the Oscar® wins for *Ben-Hur*—a biblical epic based on an 1880 novel by General Lew Wallace—include Best Actor (Charlton Heston) and Director. *The Lord of the Rings: The Return of the King* is the final film in the epic trilogy based on the works of J.R.R. Tolkien. With 11 awards, it is the most successful movie in Academy Awards® history because it won in every category in which it was nominated. Some of these wins include Best Picture, Best Director (Peter Jackson), and Best Costume Design. Some of *Titanic's* Oscars® include Cinematography, Visual Effects, and Costume Design.

Top
Moviegoing Country

United States

Each year, the average American sees about six movies. That equals about 1.53 billion admissions annually. The average ticket price in the United States is $6. In total, moviegoers spend more than $9.63 billion on trips to the big screen. In fact, Americans have spent more than $1 billion on movie tickets annually for the last 30 years. Some 475 movies are released throughout the country each year. When a new movie is released, it runs for about eight weeks in theaters and is shown on about 2,000 screens.

Top
MOVIEGOING COUNTRIES
Annual movies seen per capita

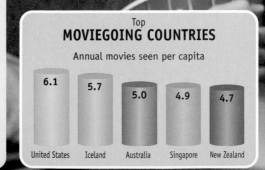

United States	Iceland	Australia	Singapore	New Zealand
6.1	5.7	5.0	4.9	4.7

Country with the
Most Movie Theaters

United States

There are more than 35,000 movie theaters with 36,600 screens throughout the country. Since the first permanent electric theater opened in 1902, Americans have flocked to the big screen. Megaplexes, or large movie theaters that show several movies at the same time, are the most popular type of theater in the country. The movie theater industry has received stiff competition in recent years, however, due to the increasing popularity of home theater systems and cable channels offering movies on demand.

Country with the
MOST MOVIE THEATERS

Number of movie theaters

United States	India	France	Germany	China
35,000	11,100	5,300	4,900	1,200

Highest
Animated Film Budget

The Polar Express

The Polar Express went into production with an unprecedented budget of $150 million. Its final production cost totaled $165 million. The film used new computer-generated technology called performance capture, giving the animation an incredibly realistic look. The animated film is based on the popular children's book about a magical train headed toward the North Pole on Christmas Eve. Several characters in the movie are voiced by Tom Hanks. The film has made more than $150 million since its release in 2004.

Highest
ANIMATED FILM BUDGETS

Budgets, in millions of US dollars

$165 M	$140 M	$137 M	$130 M	$128 M
The Polar Express, 2004	Treasure Planet, 2002	Final Fantasy: The Spirits Within, 2001	Tarzan, 1999	Dinosaur, 2000

Highest-Paid
Director/Producer

George Lucas

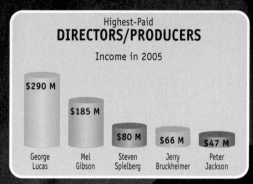

Highest-Paid
DIRECTORS/PRODUCERS
Income in 2005

$290 M	$185 M	$80 M	$66 M	$47 M
George Lucas	Mel Gibson	Steven Spielberg	Jerry Bruckheimer	Peter Jackson

Director George Lucas took home $290 million in 2005. The biggest contribution to Lucas's earnings was *Star Wars: Episode III—Revenge of the Sith*. The blockbuster movie, written by Lucas, has made more than $848 billion since its release in May 2005. Lucas wrote the first *Star Wars* movie in 1977, and has been involved in an additional five movies in that series since then. Lucas is also known for his work on the famous *Indiana Jones* movies which began in 1981 with *Raiders of the Lost Ark*.

World's Highest-Paid Actor

Arnold Schwarzenegger

For his role as T-850 in *Terminator 3: Rise of the Machines* in 2003, Arnold Schwarzenegger earned a record-shattering $30 million. Schwarzenegger reprised his role as the Terminator in the third installment of the sci-fi action movie saga that began in 1984. His first title role in a movie was *Conan the Barbarian* in 1982 for which he earned $250,000. In 1996, Schwarzenegger earned $20 million for *Jingle All the Way* (1996). By the late 1990s, his salary had increased to $25 million for movies such as *Batman & Robin* (1997), *End of Days* (1999), and *The 6th Day* (2000). In 2003, Schwarzenegger expanded his career to include politics when he was elected as the governor of California.

The World's
HIGHEST-PAID ACTORS

Salary in millions of US dollars

$30 M	$28 M	$25 M	$25 M	$25 M
Arnold Schwarzenegger, *Terminator 3*, 2003	Will Smith, *I, Robot*, 2004	Tom Cruise, *The Last Samurai*, 2003	Chris Tucker, *Rush Hour 2*, 2001	Jim Carrey, *Bruce Almighty*, 2003

World's Highest-Paid Actress

Reese Witherspoon is projected to make $29 million to star in the 2007 drama *Our Family Trouble.* Witherspoon, who was also a producer on the horror movie, plays a first-time mother who believes something is trying to destroy her family. Witherspoon's early movies included *Pleasantville* (1998), *Election* (1999), and *Cruel Intentions* (1999), but her big break came in 2001 when she portrayed Elle Woods in *Legally Blonde.* She then continued her box-office success with *Sweet Home Alabama* in 2002, which grossed more than $100 million at the box office. In 2005, she earned an Oscar® for her role as June Carter in *Walk the Line.*

Reese Witherspoon

The World's
HIGHEST-PAID ACTRESSES

Approximate salary per movie,
in millions of US dollars

$29.0 M	$25.0 M	$20.0 M	$20.0 M	$20.0 M
Reese Witherspoon, *Our Family Trouble,* 2007	Julia Roberts, *Mona Lisa Smile,* 2003	Cameron Diaz, *Charlie's Angels: Full Throttle,* 2003	Julia Roberts, *The Mexican,* 2001	Julia Roberts, *Erin Brockovich,* 2000

World's Top-Grossing Movie

Titanic

Directed by James Cameron in 1997, *Titanic* has grossed more than $600 million in the United States and more than $1.8 billion worldwide. This action-packed drama/romance is set aboard the White Star Line's lavish *RMS Titanic* in 1912. The two main characters, wealthy Rose DeWitt Bukater and the poor immigrant Jack Dawson—played by Kate Winslet and Leonardo DiCaprio—meet, fall in love, and are separated as the *Titanic* sinks into the North Atlantic on the morning of April 15, 1912.

The World's TOP-GROSSING MOVIES

Gross income, in billions and millions of US dollars

Movie	Gross
Titanic, 1997	$1.85 B
Lord of the Rings: The Return of the King, 2003	$1.12 B
Harry Potter and the Sorcerer's Stone, 2001	$977 M
Lord of the Rings: The Two Towers, 2002	$926 M
Stars Wars: Episode I— The Phantom Menace, 1999	$925 M

World's
Highest-Paid Author

Dan Brown

World-renown author Dan Brown earned $76.5 million in 2005. Most of this income was from sales of his highly successful book *The Da Vinci Code*. *The Da Vinci Code* has spent more than 150 weeks on the *New York Times* Best Seller List. It has sold more than 40 million copies worldwide and was made into a major motion picture in 2006. Three of the author's other best sellers include *Angels & Demons, Digital Fortress,* and *Deception Point*. During one week in 2004, all four of Brown's novels were on the *New York Times* Best Seller List.

The World's
HIGHEST-PAID AUTHORS

Income 2005

Dan Brown	J.K. Rowling	Nora Roberts	James Patterson	Arthur Agatston
$76.5 M	$59.1 M	$28.8 M	$27.0 M	$16.0 M

World's
Most Sucessful Artist

Pablo Picasso

Pablo Picasso's work has earned more than $1.163 billion through sales and auctions. In fact, the most expensive painting ever sold was Picasso's "Boy with a Pipe" that brought in $104 million in 2004. The Spanish painter lived from 1881 to 1973. Most of Picasso's career is divided into periods according to the colors and styles he used. First came his Blue Period (1901 to 1904), followed by his Rose Period (1905 to 1907), then his African-influenced period (1908 to 1909), leading to his Analytic Cubism Period (1909 to 1912), and finally his Synthetic Cubism Period (1912 to 1919).

The World's
MOST SUCCESSFUL ARTISTS
Total value of work, in billions and millions of US dollars

Pablo Picasso	Claude Monet	Vincent van Gogh	Paul Cézanne	Pierre-Auguste Renoir
$1.163 B	$691 M	$499 M	$425 M	$343 M

Money Records

Industry • Wealth • Most Valuable

World's
Top-Selling Car

Toyota Camry

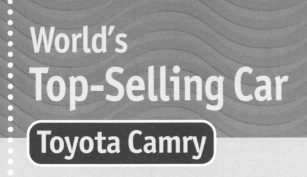

The World's
TOP-SELLING CARS
Total sold in 2005

Car	Total sold
Toyota Camry	433,703
Honda Accord	369,293
Toyota Corolla	339,732
Honda Civic	308,415
Nissan Altima	255,371

The Toyota Camry was the most popular car in 2005, with sales totaling more than 428,000 vehicles. The Camry has a standard 2.4-litre, 16-valve engine and features cruise control, keyless entry, and a state-of-the-art audio system. The Camry has also been rated as one of the safest cars on the road. In addition to front, overhead, and side-impact airbags, the car features Vehicle Skid Control brakes.

U.S. Company with the Highest Paid CEO

Yahoo!

U.S. Companies with the HIGHEST-PAID CEOs

2005 earnings in millions of US dollars

$230.6 M	$156.2 M	$124.8 M	$92.1 M	$88.7 M
Yahoo!	IAC/Inter Active Corporation	United Health Group	Forest Labs	United Technologies

Yahoo! chairman and chief executive officer Terry Semel earns $230.6 million. The sixty-three-year-old CEO is paid a $600,000 salary, but earns the remaining $229.9 million in stock gains. An executive at Warner Brothers for 24 years, Semel joined Yahoo! in May 2001. In addition to his work at Yahoo!, Semel also holds board positions with Polo Ralph Lauren Corporation, Revlon, Inc., and the Guggenheim Museum. Yahoo! is the world's largest online network of services, as well as one of the most-visited sites on the World Wide Web.

United States'
Best-Selling Cereal Brand

Cheerios

In one year, Americans spent more than $290 million on Cheerios. That amounts to about 130 million boxes in 12 months. The tasty breakfast staple makes up about 10% of the cold cereal market. Cheerioats debuted as the first ready-to-eat cereal in 1941, and changed its name to Cheerios in 1945. Some other types of Cheerios include Honey Nut Cheerios, Frosted Cheerios, Apple Cinnamon Cheerios, MultiGrain Cheerios, Team Cheerios, and Berry Burst Cheerios.

The United States'
BEST-SELLING CEREAL BRANDS
Annual sales in millions of US dollars

Cheerios	Honey Nut Cheerios	Frosted Flakes	Honey Bunches of Oats	Cinnamon Toast Crunch
$290.28 M	$247.84 M	$247.82 M	$238.94 M	$198.50 M

Country That
Spends the Most on Toys

United States

Countries That
SPEND THE MOST ON TOYS
Annual per capita spending

USA	UK	Japan	France	Germany
$123	$115	$70	$68	$65

In 2005, Americans spent an amazing $35.7 billion on toys! That's equivalent to every single person in the country buying $123 worth of toys! It's not too much of a surprise considering toys are sold practically everywhere, from grocery stores to hardware stores. Wal-Mart averages the highest toy sales with 22% of the market, followed by Toys "R" Us with 14%. The United States also leads the world in toy development, marketing, and advertising and employs more than 32,000 people in those fields.

United States'
Best-Selling Candy Brand

Hershey's Chocolate Bar

Each year, more than $82.5 million worth of Hershey's chocolate bars are sold throughout the United States. Americans eat more than 32.9 million of these bars each month, totaling almost 395 million bars a year. That's enough bars to stretch from New York City to Los Angeles more than 12 times. Hershey's bars are made in the world's largest chocolate factory that occupies 2 million square feet (185,806 sq m) of floor space. The original milk-chocolate bar was introduced in 1900, and it's main ingredients are cocoa beans, milk, and sugar.

NET WT. 1.55 OZ (43 g)

HERSHEY'S Milk Chocolate ®

The United States'
BEST-SELLING CANDY BRANDS

Annual sales in millions of US dollars

$82.52 M — Hershey's Chocolate Bars
$80.40 M — M&M's
$79.57 M — Reese's Peanut Butter Cups
$71.27 M — Snickers
$39.87 M — Kit Kat

World's Largest International Food Franchise

McDonald's

There are more than 30,500 McDonald's restaurants in the world, serving customers in 119 different countries. The company adds approximately 100 new franchises each year. About 70% of the restaurant franchises are run by local businesspeople. McDonald's serves about 50 million customers each day, about 24 million of whom are in the United States. Out of respect for local cultures, restaurants in different countries modify their menus according to religious or cultural traditions. For example, there is a kosher McDonald's in Jerusalem, and the Big Macs in India are made with lamb instead of beef.

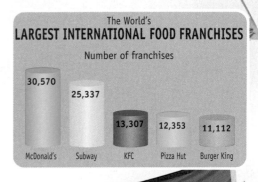

The World's
LARGEST INTERNATIONAL FOOD FRANCHISES
Number of franchises

McDonald's	Subway	KFC	Pizza Hut	Burger King
30,570	25,337	13,307	12,353	11,112

World's
Richest Woman

Lilianne Bettencourt

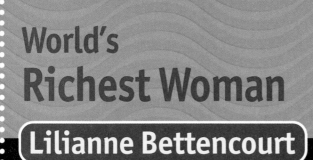

Liliane Bettencourt is the richest woman in the world with $16.0 billion. She is the only daughter of Eugene Schueller, founder of the cosmetic giant L'Oréal. In 1957, Bettencourt inherited her father's money, in addition to a controlling stake in the business. Today, L'Oréal is one of the world's most profitable cosmetics companies. A native of France, Bettencourt is the country's second-richest citizen. She has founded the Bettencourt Schueller Foundation, which grants European scientists $300,000 for research in biology or medicine.

The World's RICHEST WOMEN

Assets in billions of US dollars

Lilianne Bettencourt, France	Christy Walton, USA	Alice L. Walton, USA	Helen R. Walton, USA	Abigail Johnson, USA
$16.0 B	$15.9 B	$15.7 B	$15.6 B	$12.5 B

World's Richest Man

Bill Gates

Bill Gates is probably one of the world's most recognizable businesspeople. He is the co-founder of Microsoft—the most valuable computer software company in the world—and he is worth an incredible $50.0 billion. As Microsoft's largest individual shareholder, Gates became a billionaire on paper when the company went public in 1986. Gates has also combined his love of art and computers to create Corbis—a successful digital image archiving company. He has been very generous with his fortune. Through his Gates Foundation, he has donated billions of dollars to health research, libraries, and education.

The World's
RICHEST MEN
Assets in billions of US dollars

$50.0 B	$42.0 B	$30.0 B	$28.0 B	$23.5 B
Bill Gates, USA	Warren Buffet, USA	Carlos Slim Helú, Mexico	Ingvar Kamprad, Sweden	Lakshmi Mittal, India

World's
Poorest Country

East Timor

East Timor is a small country in Southeast Asia. It is made up of the islands of Atauro and Jaco, the eastern part of the island of Timor, and a small section of the western part of the island of Timor called Oecussi-Ambeno. The country has a gross domestic product of just $400 per capita. East Timor was formerly under the rule of Indonesia, but the islands' citizens voted for independence in 1999. This sparked a great deal of fighting between the two countries, and many of East Timor's economic resources were destroyed. Many of the citizens who had fled the country have returned, and work is underway to restore the country's profitable coffee industry.

The World's
POOREST COUNTRIES

Gross domestic product per capita in US dollars

East Timor	Somalia	Burundi	Tanzania	Ethiopia
$400	$600	$700	$700	$800

World's
Richest Country

Luxembourg

Luxembourg is a very small country in western Europe with a population of 469,000. It has a gross domestic product of $62,700 per person. The gross domestic product is calculated by dividing the annual worth of all the goods and services produced in a country by the country's population. Luxembourg's low inflation and low unemployment rates help to keep the economy solid. The industrial sector makes up a large part of the country's gross domestic product and includes products such as iron and steel, food processing, chemicals, metal products, engineering, tires, glass, and aluminum. The country's financial sector also plays a significant role in the economy, accounting for about 22% of the gross domestic product.

The World's
RICHEST COUNTRIES

Gross domestic product per capita in US dollars

Luxembourg	Norway	USA	Switzerland	Iceland
$62,700	$42,400	$41,800	$35,000	$34,600

World's Youngest Billionaire

Athina Onassis Roussel

Greek shipping tycoon Aristotle Onassis left his granddaughter well provided for. When Athina Onassis Roussel turned 18 years old in 2003, she inherited an estimated $2.7 billion in properties, including an island in the Ionian Sea, companies, artwork, and a private jet. At 21, she became president of the Athens-based Onassis Foundation and received another $2 billion. She became the only heir to the Onassis shipping fortune when her mother, Christina, died in 1988. Currently, the estate is being managed by financial advisers. Athina married Brazilian professional equestrian show jumper Alvaro de Miranda Neto in December 2005 and the newlyweds reside in Brazil.

The World's
YOUNGEST BILLIONAIRES

Age in 2007

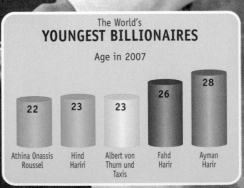

Athina Onassis Roussel	Hind Hariri	Albert von Thurn und Taxis	Fahd Harir	Ayman Harir
22	23	23	26	28

World's Most Expensive Hotel

The Mansion at the MGM Grand

Guests staying at The Mansion at the MGM Grand in Las Vegas, Nevada, pay $5,000 per night. And that's just the room—food and beverages are extra. That's about 25 times the average hotel room rate. The Mansion, which was made to look like a Florentine villa, has 29 rooms. The rooms range from 2,900 square feet (269.4 sq m) to 9,000 square feet (836.1 sq m). Each room has a butler who is on call 24 hours a day. The Mansion also features a spectacular dining room, an 800-piece art collection, a screening room to watch movies, a private pool and spa, and two chefs on call to create whatever guests would like to eat.

The World's
MOST EXPENSIVE HOTELS

Price per room, per night

$5,000	$3,217	$2,482	$2,200	$2,092
The Mansion at the MGM Grand, USA	North Island, Seychelles	Frégate Island Private, Seychelles	Singita Private Game Reserve, South Africa	Le Toiny, St. Barts

World's
Most Expensive Watch

Vacheron Constantin Tour de l'Ile

The Tour de l'Ile watch sells for $1.5 million. It was created by Vacheron Constantin—the world's oldest watchmaker. The piece was created to mark the watchmaker's 250th anniversary. It took seven years to develop the watch, and an additional three years to assemble it. The watch has 834 separate parts, making it the world's most complicated timepiece. Some of the features of the Tour de l'Ile include a perpetual calendar, a moon-phase chart, a sky chart, and the sunrise and sunset times. Only seven of these luxury watches were created.

The World's
MOST EXPENSIVE WATCHES

Price

Tour de l'Ile	Blancpain 1735	Girard-Perregaux Opera Three	Parmigiani Fleurier Toric Corrector Quantième Perpétual	Roger Dubuis Excalibur EX 08
$1.5 M	$839,000	$532,000	$477,000	$450,000

United States'
Most Valuable Movie Franchise

Star Wars

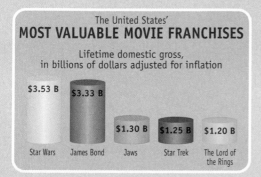

The United States'
MOST VALUABLE MOVIE FRANCHISES

Lifetime domestic gross,
in billions of dollars adjusted for inflation

$3.53 B	$3.33 B			
		$1.30 B	$1.25 B	$1.20 B
Star Wars	James Bond	Jaws	Star Trek	The Lord of the Rings

The Star Wars movie franchise is the most valuable in the United States, with a combined domestic gross of $3.53 billion. Of the six movies in the franchise, Star Wars has brought in the most money with $461 million. Combined, the Star Wars movies have sold a total of more than 560 million tickets. Written, produced, and directed by George Lucas, the first Star Wars movie opened in 1977. Some of the movies' biggest stars include Harrison Ford, Liam Neeson, Samuel L. Jackson, Natalie Portman, and Ewan McGregor.

209

World's
Most Expensive Restaurant

Aragawa

Diners eating at Aragawa in Tokyo, Japan, had better bring their wallets—the average meal per person totals $277! The restaurant was the country's first steak house, and it is famous for its Kobe beef. The Sumiyaki (charcoal-broiled steak) is served only with pepper and mustard, and is one of the most popular dishes at Aragawa. The formal restaurant is decorated with dark wood paneling and a sparkling chandelier to create a special atmosphere for guests.

The World's
MOST EXPENSIVE RESTAURANTS

Average cost of a meal

Aragawa, Tokyo	Eigensinn Farm, Toronto	Arpège, Paris	Sketch, London	Petermann's Kunststuben, Zurich
$277	$213	$211	$176	$151

World's
Most Valuable Baseball

Mark McGwire's 70th Home Run Baseball

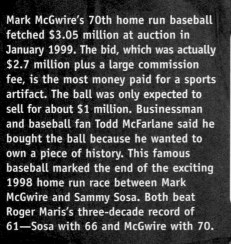

Mark McGwire's 70th home run baseball fetched $3.05 million at auction in January 1999. The bid, which was actually $2.7 million plus a large commission fee, is the most money paid for a sports artifact. The ball was only expected to sell for about $1 million. Businessman and baseball fan Todd McFarlane said he bought the ball because he wanted to own a piece of history. This famous baseball marked the end of the exciting 1998 home run race between Mark McGwire and Sammy Sosa. Both beat Roger Maris's three-decade record of 61—Sosa with 66 and McGwire with 70.

The World's
MOST VALUABLE BASEBALLS
Price paid at auction, in US dollars

$3.05 M	$517,500	$150,000	$125,500	$106,600
McGwire's 70th Home Run Baseball	Bonds' 73rd Home Run Baseball	Sosa's 66th Home Run Baseball	Ruth's First Yankee Stadium Home Run Baseball	Cub's 2003 Playoffs Foul Ball

World's Most Valuable Production Car

Saleen S7

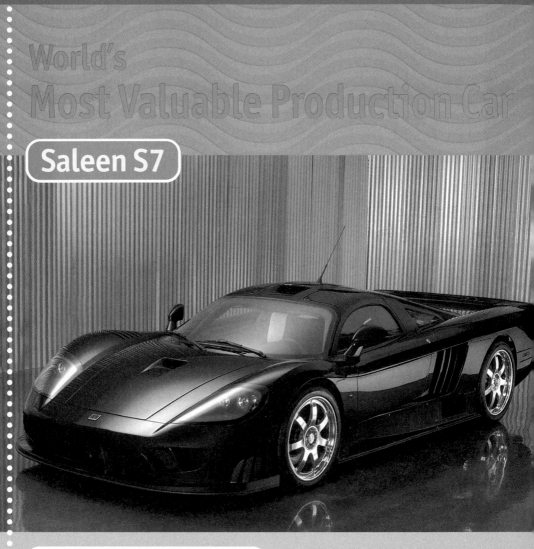

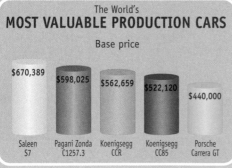

The World's
MOST VALUABLE PRODUCTION CARS

Base price

$670,389	$598,025	$562,659	$522,120	$440,000
Saleen S7	Pagani Zonda C1257.3	Koenigsegg CCR	Koenigsegg CC85	Porsche Carrera GT

The base price for a Saleen S7 is a cool $670,389. That's about four times more than the price of the average home in the United States! The Saleen S7 actually costs about $115,000 less in the United States because the car was designed to meet the country's automobile regulations. When the car is modified to meet European safety and performance regulations, the price goes up. The Saleen S7 has a V8 engine with 750 horsepower—the highest horsepower of any car in the United States. It can accelerate from 0 to 60 in under three seconds, and can reach a top speed of more than 200 miles (322 km) per hour. Each car is custom-built for its owner.

Science Records

Computers • Technology • Solar System
Space • Video Games • Vehicles

World's Most-Visited Web Site

Time Warner Network

The Web Sites with the
MOST VISITORS

Number of new users each month, in millions

118.5 M	118.2 M	112.2 M	79.9 M	64.1 M
Time Warner Network	Yahoo!	MSN	Google	eBay

Each month, approximately 118.5 million people visit the Web sites in the Time Warner network. The company includes AOL; HBO; Warner Bros.™; Time, Inc.; New Line Cinema; Turner Broadcasting System; and Time Warner Cable. The majority of the visitors—some 110 million people—visit AOL. Some of the sites affiliated with AOL include Netscape, MapQuest, Moviefone, and AOL Music Now. Warner Brothers Pictures also has Web sites for all of its movies, and some of the studio's big hits include *Batman Begins*, *Charlie and the Chocolate Factory* and *Harry Potter and the Goblet of Fire*.

Country with the
Most Internet Users

United States

The number of Internet users has doubled in the last five years. Americans now account for 20% of users worldwide. In the United States, more than 200 million people are surfing the World Wide Web. That's more than 50% of the population. Throughout the nation, the largest number of Internet users are women between the ages of 18 and 54, closely followed by men in that age-group. Teens ages 12 to 17 are the third-largest Internet-using group. The average Internet user spends about 15 hours online per week.

The Countries with the
MOST INTERNET USERS
Users in millions

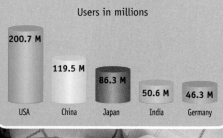

USA	China	Japan	India	Germany
200.7 M	119.5 M	86.3 M	50.6 M	46.3 M

World's
Fastest Computer

BlueGene

BlueGene is the most powerful supercomputer in the world and is capable of performing 280.6 trillion calculations per second. That's about the same as every person in the world doing 40,000 calculations in a second. Housed in the Lawrence Livermore National Laboratory in California, BlueGene is made up of 131,000 processors and is three times faster than the next-fastest computer. BlueGene is used by the government to study classified information.

The World's
FASTEST COMPUTERS

Calculations per second, in trillions

BlueGene	BGW	ASC Purple	Columbia	Thunderbird
280.6 T	91.3 T	63.4 T	51.9 T	38.3 T

World's
Most-Visited Shopping Site

eBay

When online shoppers are looking to spend money, the majority check eBay first. With 64.1 million visitors each month, eBay truly is the World's Online Marketplace®. The company was founded in 1995, and the online auction and shopping Web site attracts sellers and bidders from all over the world. Each year, millions of items—including spectacular treasures, unusual services, and even worthless junk—trade hands. Some of the most expensive sales include a Grumman Gulfstream II Jet for $4.9 million and a 1909 Honus Wagner baseball card for $1.65 million.

The World's
MOST-VISITED SHOPPING SITES

Visitors who visited at least once
during June 2005, in millions

64.1 M	40.1 M	22.7 M	19.1 M	18.5 M
eBay.com	Amazon.com	Walmart.com	Shopping.com	Shopzilla.com

Country with the
Highest Internet Use

Iceland

Iceland rates number one in Internet usage, with 75.9% of its citizens surfing the web. That means that about 225,000 Icelandic people log on to the Internet. The Internet was first available in Iceland in 1986, and connections grew steadily each year. Between 2000 and 2005, Iceland's Internet usage grew more than 34%. Approximately 45,000 households have broadband Internet connections. Almost 90% of the people accessing the Internet are between the ages of 16 and 24. The most popular online activity in Iceland is shopping.

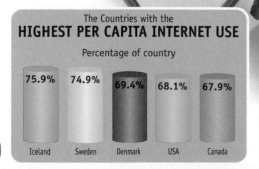

The Countries with the
HIGHEST PER CAPITA INTERNET USE
Percentage of country

Iceland	Sweden	Denmark	USA	Canada
75.9%	74.9%	69.4%	68.1%	67.9%

Country with the
Most Robots

Japan

There are more than 350,000 robots currently moving around in Japan. Many of the country's largest industrial companies—including Honda Motor, Toyota Motor, and Sony—are assembling these lifelike creatures. Many of these robots are being designed to interact with and care for people. With Japan's aging population, researchers have predicted that the market for these robots will grow to about $10 billion in the next 10 years. Some of Japan's newest robots read stories to children, cheer up and assist hospital patients, play music and dance, and recommend food choices based on medical history.

The Countries with the
MOST ROBOTS

Number of operational robots

Japan	Germany	USA	Italy	South Korea
350,169	105,217	103,515	46,881	44,265

Country with the
Most Cell Phone Accounts

Luxembourg

Almost the entire population of Luxembourg is taking advantage of wireless communication, with 106 cell phone accounts per every 100 people. Many people have more than one cell phone account. Luxembourg's healthy economy and growing business and financial sectors thrive on the ability to communicate instantly. SES Global—the world's largest satellite company—is located in Luxembourg and provides cell phone services to 94 million people throughout Europe.

The Countries with the
MOST CELL PHONE ACCOUNTS

Cell phone accounts per 100 people

Luxembourg	Italy	Iceland	Czech Republic	Israel
106.1	101.8	96.6	96.5	95.8

Country with the
Most Cell Phone Subscribers

United States

More than 182 million people in the United States subscribe to cell phone service. That's about 62% of the country's population, and about 14% of total cell phone subscribers worldwide. As cell phone service improves and the costs go down, more and more Americans are abandoning traditional landlines in favor of wireless communication. And with the wide range of services offered by cell phone companies—including text and photo messaging, Internet accessibility, and standard voice service—many Americans rely on their phones to plan and manage their social and business schedules. Each year, cell phone sales and service totals about $10 billion.

The Countries with the
MOST CELL PHONE SUBSCRIBERS

Subscribers, in millions

United States	Japan	Germany	Italy	United Kingdom
182.1 M	86.7 M	64.8 M	55.9 M	49.7 M

Country That
Watches the Most TV

Thailand

Each week, each person in Thailand watches an average of 22.4 hours of television. That totals 48.5 days a year—more than a month and a half—devoted to TV viewing. Television is the most popular medium in the country, and more than 80% of the Thai people get their news from that source. Thailand's six terrestrial television stations are controlled by the military or the government. There are also several independent cable and satellite providers in the country.

The Countries that
WATCH THE MOST TV

Average TV viewing, in hours per week

Thailand	Philippines	Egypt	Turkey	Indonesia
22.4	21.0	20.9	20.2	19.7

Planet with the Most Moons

Jupiter

Jupiter—the fifth planet from the Sun—has 63 moons. Most of these moons—also called satellites—do not resemble traditional moons. Most are quite small, measuring from just .62 miles (.99 km) to 4 miles (6.4 km) across. Jupiter's four largest moons are Ganymede, Europa, Io, and Callisto. The moons travel in an elliptical, or egg-shaped, orbit in the opposite direction that Jupiter rotates. Astronomers believe these irregular moons formed somewhere else in the solar system and were pulled into Jupiter's atmosphere when they passed too close to the planet. Astronomers are constantly finding new moons for several of the planets, partly because of the highly-sensitive telescopes and cameras now available to them.

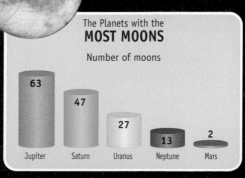

The Planets with the
MOST MOONS

Number of moons

Jupiter	Saturn	Uranus	Neptune	Mars
63	47	27	13	2

Star That Is
Closest to Earth

Proxima Centauri

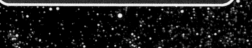

Proxima Centauri is approximately 24.7925 trillion miles (39.9233 trillion km) from Earth, making it our closest star other than the Sun. Light from the star reaches Earth in just 4.2 years. It is the third member of the Alpha Centauri triple system. This tiny red dwarf star is about 10% of the Sun's mass and .006% as bright. The surface temperature is thought to be about 3,000° Fahrenheit (1,650° C). More accurate measures of the star's size are not possible because it is so small. But these measurements are enough to cause scientists to believe that Proxima Centauri does not have any planets orbiting it that support life. If planets did exist, they would be too cold and dark for life-forms to exist.

The Stars that are
CLOSEST TO EARTH

Distance in trillions of miles/kilometers

Proxima Centauri	Alpha Centauri	Barnard's Star	Wolf 359	Lalande 21185
24.8 T mi. 39.9 T km.	25.6 T mi. 41.2 T km.	35.1 T mi. 56.6 T km.	45.5 T mi. 73.3 T km.	48.3 T mi. 77.8 T km.

Planet with the Hottest Surface

Venus

The surface temperature on Venus can reach a sizzling 870° Fahrenheit (465° C). That's approximately 19 times hotter than the average temperature on Earth. About every 19 months, Venus is closer to Earth than any other planet in the solar system. Venus is covered by a dense atmosphere. There are clouds made of acid, hurricane-strength winds, and lots of lightning. This makes it difficult to know what features are on its surface. The atmosphere also reflects a great deal of sunlight. At times, Venus is the third-brightest object in the sky, after the Sun and the Moon.

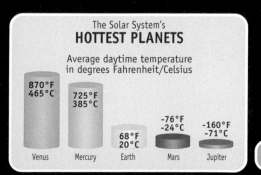

The Solar System's
HOTTEST PLANETS

Average daytime temperature in degrees Fahrenheit/Celsius

Venus	Mercury	Earth	Mars	Jupiter
870°F 465°C	725°F 385°C	68°F 20°C	-76°F -24°C	-160°F -71°C

Planet with the
Fastest Orbit

Mercury

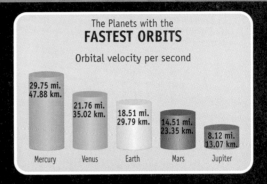

The Planets with the
FASTEST ORBITS

Orbital velocity per second

29.75 mi.
47.88 km.

21.76 mi.
35.02 km.

18.51 mi.
29.79 km.

14.51 mi.
23.35 km.

8.12 mi.
13.07 km.

Mercury Venus Earth Mars Jupiter

Mercury orbits the Sun at about 30 miles (48 km) per second. At this astonishing speed, the planet can circle the Sun in about 88 Earth days. On Mercury, a solar day (the time from one sunrise to the next) lasts about 176 Earth days. Mercury's surface resembles that of the Earth's moon, with flat plains, steep cliffs, and craters. Even though Mercury is the closest planet to the Sun, the temperature on the planet can change drastically. During the day, it can reach as high as 840° Fahrenheit (448° C), but at night, temperatures can fall to around -300° Fahrenheit (-149° C)!

Solar System's
Largest Planet

Jupiter has a radius of 43,441 miles (69,909 km)—that's almost 11 times larger than Earth's radius. In fact, the Earth could fit inside Jupiter more than 1,000 times! Jupiter is about 480 million miles (772 million km) from the Sun. It takes almost 12 Earth years for Jupiter to make one complete circle around the Sun. Although it is very large, Jupiter has a high rotation speed. One Jupiter day is less than 10 Earth hours long. That is the shortest solar day in the solar system.

The Solar System's
LARGEST PLANETS
Mean radius in miles/kilometers

Jupiter	Saturn	Uranus	Neptune	Earth
43,411 mi. 69,863 km.	36,184 mi. 59,246 km.	15,759 mi. 25,361 km.	15,301 mi. 24,624 km.	3,959 mi. 6,371 km.

Planet with the Most Rings

Saturn

Scientists estimate that approximately 1,000 rings circle Saturn—hundreds more than any other planet. This ring system is only about 328 feet (100 m) thick, but reaches a diameter of 167,780 miles (270,000 km). The three major rings around the planet are named A, B, and C. Although they appear solid, Saturn's rings are made of particles of planet and satellite matter that range in size from about 1 to 15 feet (.3 to 4.5 m). Because of the rings' brightness, scientists believe they are not as old as the planet they circle. Saturn, which is the sixth planet from the Sun, is the solar system's second-largest planet in size and mass.

The Planets
WITH THE MOST RINGS

Number of rings

Saturn	Uranus	Neptune	Jupiter
1,000	11	6	1

Planet with the Largest Moon

Jupiter

Ganymede is the largest moon of both Jupiter and the solar system. It has a radius of 1,635 miles (2,631 km) and a diameter of 3,280 miles (5,626 km). That is almost 2.5 times larger than Earth's moon. The moon is approximately 1.4 million miles (2.25 million km) away from Jupiter and has an orbital period of about seven days. It is probably made up mostly of rock and ice. It also has lava flows, mountains, and valleys. Many of the moon's large craters were caused by collisions with comets. Ganymede has both light and dark areas that give it a textured appearance. Ganymede was discovered by Galileo Galilei and Simon Marius almost 400 years ago.

The Planets with the
LARGEST MOONS

Radius in miles/kilometers

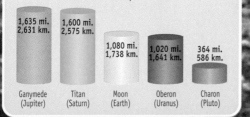

1,635 mi. 2,631 km.	1,600 mi. 2,575 km.	1,080 mi. 1,738 km.	1,020 mi. 1,641 km.	364 mi. 586 km.
Ganymede (Jupiter)	Titan (Saturn)	Moon (Earth)	Oberon (Uranus)	Charon (Pluto)

Planet with the
Longest Year

Pluto

If you think a year on planet Earth is a long time, don't travel to Pluto any time soon! One year on Pluto is equivalent to 247.7 years on Earth, which means that a single day on Pluto is equal to 6.4 days here. This is because Pluto's location ranges from 2.8 to 4.6 billion miles (4.4 to 7.4 billion km) away from the Sun, approximately 39 times farther from the Sun than Earth. Pluto is also the least massive planet in the solar system. In 2006, NASA launched the New Horizons spacecraft to study Pluto and its moon, Charon. It is expected to reach the planet by 2015 and record Pluto's temperature, atmosphere and surface composition.

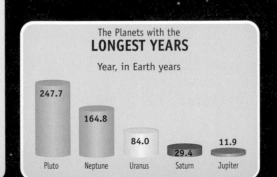

The Planets with the
LONGEST YEARS

Year, in Earth years

Pluto	Neptune	Uranus	Saturn	Jupiter
247.7	164.8	84.0	29.4	11.9

World's
Brightest Galaxy

Large Magellanic Cloud

The Large Magellanic Cloud (LMC) is the brightest galaxy in the universe with an apparent magnitude of 0.91. First noted by the explorer Ferdinand Magellan in 1519, the LMC is a small galaxy in the southern constellations. Approximately 160,000 light-years from Earth, the LMC is an irregular dwarf galaxy that orbits the Milky Way. It is full of gas and dust, and new stars are continually forming within it. It is approximately one-twentieth the size of Earth's galaxy and contains about one-tenth the number of stars.

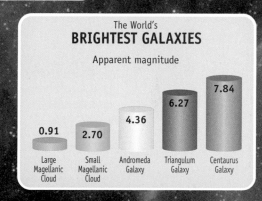

The World's
BRIGHTEST GALAXIES

Apparent magnitude

0.91	2.70	4.36	6.27	7.84
Large Magellanic Cloud	Small Magellanic Cloud	Andromeda Galaxy	Triangulum Galaxy	Centaurus Galaxy

Solar System's Smallest Planet

Pluto

Pluto has a radius of about 707 miles (1,138 km). That's about two-thirds the size of the Moon and about half the width of the United States. Pluto is also the coldest planet, with an average surface temperature of -370° Fahrenheit (-233° Celsius). The planet appears to have polar ice caps that extend halfway to its equator. It is normally the farthest planet from the Sun, but its unusual orbit brings it closer than Neptune about every 250 years. The last time this happened was in 1979, when Pluto became the eighth planet for 20 years. First noticed in 1930, Pluto was the last planet to be discovered in our solar system.

Pluto and its moon, Charon

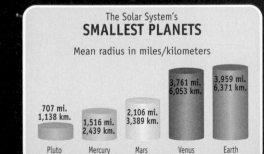

The Solar System's
SMALLEST PLANETS

Mean radius in miles/kilometers

Pluto	Mercury	Mars	Venus	Earth
707 mi. 1,138 km.	1,516 mi. 2,439 km.	2,106 mi. 3,389 km.	3,761 mi. 6,053 km.	3,959 mi. 6,371 km.

World's
Longest Space Walk

Susan Helms and James Voss

The World's
LONGEST SPACE WALKS

Length of space walk, in hours and minutes

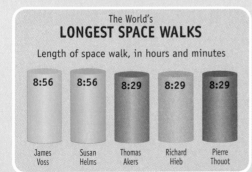

8:56	8:56	8:29	8:29	8:29
James Voss	Susan Helms	Thomas Akers	Richard Hieb	Pierre Thouot

Susan Helms and James Voss each completed a space walk that lasted 8 hours and 56 minutes on March 11, 2001. The two astronauts spent the time working on the International Space Station. They prepped a shuttle docking tunnel which needed to be moved to make room for a cargo carrier. The astronauts also attached a mounting platform that would eventually support the station's robotic arm. And even though the space walk was the longest in NASA history, the astronauts could not perform some maintenance and it was rescheduled for a future mission.

233

Galaxy
Closest to Earth

Canis Major Dwarf

Stream of the
Canis Major galaxy

Sun

Canis Major
Galaxy

Milky Way

The Canis Major Dwarf Galaxy is the Milky Way's closest neighbor, located just 42,000 light-years from Earth. The small galaxy was just discovered by astronomers from France, Italy, the UK, and Australia in 2003. The astronomers used infrared light to see past the dust in the Milky Way. This study picked up the galaxy's cool, red stars that shine brightly in infrared light. Astronomers believe that the Canis Major Dwarf is gradually being ripped apart by the Milky Way's gravitational pull.

234

The Galaxies
CLOSEST TO EARTH

Distance from Earth, in light-years

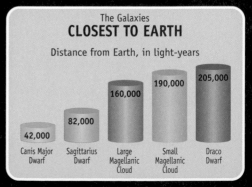

Canis Major Dwarf	Sagittarius Dwarf	Large Magellanic Cloud	Small Magellanic Cloud	Draco Dwarf
42,000	82,000	160,000	190,000	205,000

World's
Best-Selling Video Game Ever

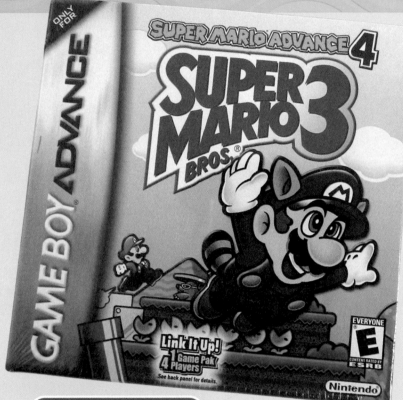

Super Mario Bros.™ 3

The World's
BEST-SELLING VIDEO GAMES EVER

Sales in millions of units since game's release

17.3 M	11.1 M	11.0 M	8.5 M	8.0 M
Super Mario Bros. 3	Super Mario Land 2	Gran Turismo 3	Gran Turismo 2	Super Mario Kart

Since its release in Japan in 1988, Super Mario Bros. 3 has sold more than 17.3 million copies around the world. The game, which was created by Nintendo, was later released in the United States in 1990 and in Europe in 1991. Similar to the first two games in the series, players help Mario and Luigi battle King Bowser to win magic wands and save Princess Toadstool. But, this version gave the game's hero special powers when he put on the raccoon, frog, or tanooki suits. It was directed by Shigeru Miyamoto, and the music was composed by Koji Kondo.

World's
Fastest Production Motorcycle

Suzuki GSX1300R Hayabusa

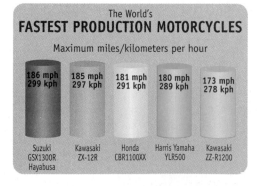

The World's
FASTEST PRODUCTION MOTORCYCLES

Maximum miles/kilometers per hour

186 mph 299 kph	185 mph 297 kph	181 mph 291 kph	180 mph 289 kph	173 mph 278 kph
Suzuki GSX1300R Hayabusa	Kawasaki ZX-12R	Honda CBR1100XX	Harris Yamaha YLR500	Kawasaki ZZ-R1200

This sleek speed machine, which is named after one of the world's fastest birds, is able to reach a maximum speed of 186 miles (299 km) per hour. That's about three times faster than the speed limit on most major highways. The 2006 Hayabusa features a 1299-cc, liquid-cooled DOHC engine. Its aerodynamic shape, four-cylinder engine, and six-speed transmission make the bike very popular with motorcycle enthusiasts. In 2001, motorcycle manufacturers set a guideline stating that no new production motorcycles will have a top speed above 186 miles (299 km) per hour, for safety reasons.

World's Fastest Land Vehicle

Thrust SSC

The Thrust SSC, which stands for supersonic car, reached a speed of 763 miles (1,228 km) per hour on October 15, 1997. At that speed, a car could make it from San Francisco to New York City in less than 4 hours. The Thrust SSC is propelled by two jet engines capable of 110,000 horsepower. It has the same power as 1,000 Ford Escorts or 145 Formula One race cars. The Thrust SSC runs on jet fuel, using about 5 gallons (19 l) per second. It only takes approximately five seconds for this supersonic car to reach its top speed. It is 54 feet (16.5 m) long and weighs 7 tons (6.4 t).

The Vehicles with the FASTEST SPEEDS ON LAND

Speed in miles/kilometers per hour

Vehicle	Speed
Thrust SSC, 1997	763 mph / 1,228 kph
Thrust 2, 1983	633 mph / 1,019 kph
Blue Flame, 1970	622 mph / 1,001 kph
Spirit of America, 1965	600 mph / 966 kph
Green Monster, 1965	576 mph / 927 kph

237

World's
Fastest Passenger Train

MagLev

The superspeedy MagLev train in China carries passengers from Pudong financial district to Pudong International Airport at an average speed of 243 miles (391 km) per hour. The train reaches a top speed of 267 miles (430 km) per hour about 4 minutes into the trip. The 8-minute train ride replaces a 45-minute car trip. The MagLev, which is short for magnet levitation, actually floats in the air just above the track. Tiny magnets are used to suspend the train, and larger ones are used to pull it forward. The German-built train began commercial operation in 2004.

The World's
FASTEST PASSENGER TRAINS

Average speed in miles/kilometers per hour

Maglev, China	Nozomi, Japan	TGV, France	Acela Express, USA	TGV Thalys, International
243.0 mph 391.2 kph	162.6 mph 261.7 kph	158.0 mph 255.7 kph	150.0 mph 241.0 kph	131.2 mph 211.1 kph

MLU 002N

World's Fastest Production Car

Bugatti Veyron

The World's FASTEST PRODUCTION CARS

Maximum miles/kilometers per hour

253 mph 407 kph	245 mph 395 kph	242 mph 390 kph	240 mph 386 kph	223 mph 359 kph
Bugati Veyron	Koenigsegg CCR	Koenigsegg CC85	McLaren F1	Saleen S7

The Volkswagen Bugatti Veyron can cruise along at a top speed of 253 miles (407 km) per hour. In fact, it can reach 62 miles (100 km) per hour in just 2 seconds, and accelerate to 186 miles (300 km) per hour in only 14 seconds. That's faster than a Formula One race car! The seven-speed semi-manual transmission takes less than a quarter of a second to change gears. The Bugati Veyron is powered by an 8.0-liter W-16 engine. This ultimate sports car sells for about $1.3 million, and only 300 of them will be produced. Buyers can also opt to jazz up their new Veyron by adding two one-carat diamonds to the speedometer.

EB 18/4 "Veyron"

BUGATTI

World's Largest Cruise Ship

Freedom of the Seas

FREEDOM of the SEAS

The World's LARGEST CRUISE SHIPS

Length

1,132 ft. 345 m.	1,132 ft. 345 m.	1,020 ft. 311 m.	1,020 ft. 311 m.	1,020 ft. 311 m.
Freedom of the Seas	Queen Mary 2	Voyager of the Seas	Adventure of the Seas	Explorer of the Seas

Royal Caribbean's newest ocean liner, *The Freedom of the Seas*, weighs 160,000 tons (145,150 t)—about the same as 80,000 automobiles. The giant luxury ship measures 1,112 feet (339 m) long and 185 feet (56 m) wide. It can accommodate 3,600 guests in its 1,800 rooms. Some of the amenities that guests can enjoy include a sports pool, a surfing pool, an ice-skating rink, and a giant rock-climbing wall. The 445-foot (136-m) Royal Promenade features shopping, dining, and nightly street parades. The ship made its maiden voyage in May 2006 sails to Caribbean destinations.

World's Biggest Monster Truck

The Bigfoot 5 truly is a monster—it measures 15.4 feet (4.7 m) high! That's about three times the height of an average car. Bigfoot 5 has 10-foot- (3-m-) high Firestone Tundra tires each weighing 2,400 pounds (1,088 kg), giving the truck a total weight of about 38,000 pounds (17,236 kg). The giant wheels were from an arctic snow train operated in Alaska by the US Amy in the 1950s. This modified 1996 Ford F250 pickup truck is owned by Bob Chandler of St. Louis, Missouri. The great weight of this monster truck makes it too large to race.

Bigfoot 5

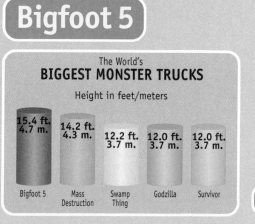

The World's
BIGGEST MONSTER TRUCKS

Height in feet/meters

Bigfoot 5	Mass Destruction	Swamp Thing	Godzilla	Survivor
15.4 ft. 4.7 m.	14.2 ft. 4.3 m.	12.2 ft. 3.7 m.	12.0 ft. 3.7 m.	12.0 ft. 3.7 m.

World's
Lightest Jet

BD-5J Microjet

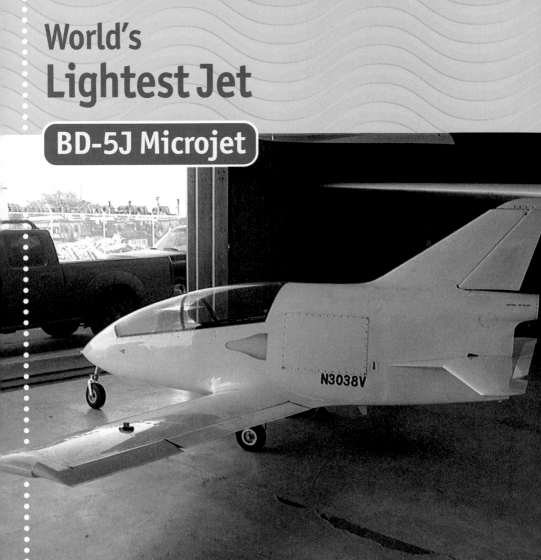

N3038V

The BD-5J Microjet weighs only 358.8 pounds (162.7 kg), making it the lightest jet in the world. At only 12 feet (3.7 m) in length, it is one of the smallest as well. This tiny jet has a height of 5.6 feet (1.7 m) and a wingspan of 17 feet (5.2 m). The Microjet uses a TRS-18 turbojet engine. It can reach a top speed of 320 miles (514.9 km) per hour, but can only carry 32 gallons (121 l) of fuel at a time. A new BD-5J costs around $200,000. This high-tech gadget was flown by James Bond in the movie *Octopussy*, and it is also occasionally used by the U.S. military.

The World's
LIGHTEST JETS

Weight in pounds/kilograms

358.8 lb. 162.7 kg.	374.0 lb. 169.6 kg.	412.0 lb. 186.9 kg.	465.0 lb. 210.9 kg.	5,600 lb. 2,540 kg.
BD-5J Microjet	Cri-Cri Jet	Silver Bullet	SMART-1	McDonnell XF-85 Goblin

World's
Fastest Plane

X-43A

The World's
FASTEST PLANES

Speed in miles/kilometers per hour

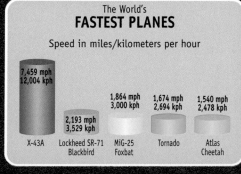

7,459 mph 12,004 kph		1,864 mph 3,000 kph	1,674 mph 2,694 kph	1,540 mph 2,478 kph
	2,193 mph 3,529 kph			
X-43A	Lockheed SR-71 Blackbird	MiG-25 Foxbat	Tornado	Atlas Cheetah

NASA's experimental X-43A plane reached a top speed of Mach 9.8—or more than nine times the speed of sound—on a test flight over the Pacific Ocean in November 2004. The X-43A was mounted on top of a Pegasus rocket booster and was carried into the sky by a B-52 aircraft. The booster was then fired, taking the X-43A about 110,000 feet (33,530 m) above the ground. The rocket was detached from the unmanned X-43A, and the plane flew unassisted for several minutes. At this rate of 7,459 miles (12,004 km) per hour, a plane could circle the Earth in just over three and a half hours!

World's
Fastest Roller Coaster

Kingda Ka

Kingda Ka—the newest coaster at Six Flags Great Adventure in Jackson, New Jersey—can launch riders straight up a track at a top speed of 128 miles (206 km) per hour. This hydraulic launch coaster reaches its top speed in less than 4 seconds. Kingda Ka is also the world's tallest rollercoaster at 456 feet (139 m). In addition to the horizontal rocket that starts the ride, the coaster also features a few breathtaking drops and spiral turns. The 50-second-long ride cost $25 million to build and debuted during the 2005 season.

The World's
FASTEST ROLLER COASTERS

Speed in miles per hour/kilometers per hour

128 mph 206 kph	120 mph 193 kph	106 mph 172 kph	100 mph 161 kph	100 mph 161 kph
Kingda Ka, USA	Top Thrill Dragster, USA	Dodonpa, Japan	Superman the Escape, USA	Tower of Terror, Australia

U.S. Records

Alabama to Wyoming

State with the
Oldest Mardi Gras Celebration

Alabama

The United States'
OLDEST MARDI GRAS CELEBRATIONS

Year celebration began

1831	1835	1842	1844	1867
Mobile, Alabama	New Orleans, Louisiana	Lafayette, Louisiana	Pensacola, Florida	Galveston, Texas

People in Mobile, Alabama, have been celebrating Mardi Gras since 1703, but did not have an official parade event until 1831. After a brief hiatus during the Civil War, the celebrations started back up in 1866 and have been growing ever since. Today, some 100,000 people gather in Mobile to enjoy the 22 parades that take place during the two weeks that lead up to Mardi Gras. On the biggest day—Fat Tuesday—six parades wind through the downtown waterfront, with floats and costumed dancers. But at the stroke of midnight, the partying stops and plans for next year begin.

State with the
Largest National Forest

Alaska

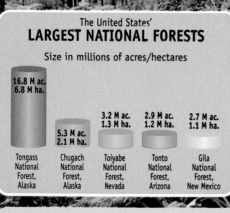

The United States'
LARGEST NATIONAL FORESTS

Size in millions of acres/hectares

**16.8 M ac.
6.8 M ha.**

**5.3 M ac.
2.1 M ha.**

**3.2 M ac.
1.3 M ha.**

**2.9 M ac.
1.2 M ha.**

**2.7 M ac.
1.1 M ha.**

Tongass National Forest, Alaska

Chugach National Forest, Alaska

Toiyabe National Forest, Nevada

Tonto National Forest, Arizona

Gila National Forest, New Mexico

The Tongass National Forest covers approximately 16.8 million acres (6.8 million ha) in Southeast Alaska. That's about the same size as West Virginia. It is also home to the world's largest temperate rain forest. Some of the forest's trees are more than 700 years old. About 11,000 miles (17,703 km) of shoreline are inside the park. Some of the animals that live in the forest include bears, salmon, and wolves. The world's largest concentration of bald eagles also spend the fall and winter here on the Chilkat River.

State with the Country's
Sunniest Place

Arizona

The little town of Yuma, Arizona, enjoys bright, sunny days approximately 90% of the year. That means that the sun is shining about 328 days out of each year! Yuma is located in southwestern Arizona near the borders of California and Mexico. Although the temperatures are normally in the 70s year-round, the dry desert air keeps the humidity low. And this sunny spot is drawing a crowd—Yuma is the third-fastest growing area in the United States.

Some of the United States'
SUNNIEST PLACES
Percentage of sunny days per year

Yuma, Arizona	Redding, California	Scottsdale, Arizona	Las Vegas, Nevada	El Paso, Texas
90%	88%	86%	85%	84%

State with the
Largest Retail Headquarters

Wal-Mart—headquartered in Bentonville, Arkansas—logged $312.4 billion in sales in 2005. The company was founded in 1962 by Arkansas native Sam Walton, who saw his small variety stores grow into giant grocery stores, membership warehouse clubs, and deep-discount warehouse outlets. Walton's original store in Bentonville now serves as the company's visitor center. Each year, the company gives back some of what it earns—in 2005 Wal-Mart contributed $170 million to nonprofit organizations.

The United States'
LARGEST RETAIL HEADQUARTERS

2005 sales, in billions of US dollars

$312.4 B	$81.5 B	$56.4 B	$55.0 B	$52.6 B
Wal-Mart, Arkansas	The Home Depot, Georgia	Kroger, Ohio	Sears Roebuck, Illinois	Target, Minnesota

State with the
Highest Avocado Production

California

The United States'
TOP AVOCADO PRODUCERS
Production in tons/metric tons

183.2 tons
166.2 t.

9.8 tons
8.9 t.

3.9 tons
2.5 t.

California   Florida   Hawaii

California is the country's top producer of avocados—harvesting about 183.4 tons (166.2 t), or 93% of the United States' crop. There are approximately 6,000 growers in the state, and each farm is around 10 acres (4.1 ha) in size. In one year, a single avocado tree can produce some 60 pounds (27.2 kg), or about 120 pieces, of fruit. Because of its warm coastal climate, the state can grow avocados year round. The town of Fallbrook is known as the Avocado Capital of the World and hosts the annual Avocado Festival each year.

State's Baseball Team with the Highest Seasonal Attendance

Colorado

In 1993, the seasonal attendance for the Colorado Rockies was an impressive 4.48 million fans. The Rockies finished up their inaugural season in October of the same year with the most wins by a National League expansion team. The Rockies played at Mile High Stadium for their first two years. The team moved to Denver's Coors Field in 1995. The new park was designed to have 43,800 seats, but with such high attendance at Mile High Stadium, architects reworked the plans to include 50,200 seats. The team proceeded to sell out 203 consecutive games.

Baseball Teams with the
HIGHEST SEASONAL ATTENDANCE

Seasonal attendance, in millions

Colorado Rockies, 1993	New York Yankees, 2004	Los Angeles Dodgers, 2004	Atlanta Braves, 1997	Cleveland Indians, 2000
4.48 M	3.77 M	3.48 M	3.46 M	3.45 M

State with the Oldest Theme Park

Connecticut

Lake Compounce in Bristol, Connecticut, first opened as a picnic park in 1846. The park's first electric roller coaster, the Green Dragon, was introduced in 1914 and cost 10 cents per ride. It was replaced by the WildCat in 1927, and the wooden coaster still operates today. In 1996 the park got a $50 million upgrade, which included the thrilling new roller coaster Boulder Dash. It is the only coaster to be built into a mountainside. Another $3.3 million was spent on upgrades in 2005, including an 800-foot (244-meter) lazy river.

The United States'
OLDEST THEME PARKS

Years of establishment

1846	1870	1878	1879	1894
Lake Compounce, Connecticut	Cedar Point, Ohio	Idlewood Park, Pennsylvania	Seabreeze Park, New Jersey	Lakemont Park, Pennsylvania

State with the Largest
Pumpkin-Throwing Contest

Delaware

Each year approximately 30,000 people gather in Sussex County, Delaware, for the annual World Championship Punkin Chunkin. More than 70 teams compete during the three-day festival to see who can chuck their pumpkin the farthest. Each team constructs a machine that has a mechanical or compressed-air firing device—no explosives are allowed. The farthest a pumpkin has traveled during the championship is 4,434 feet (1,352 m), or the length of twelve football fields. The total combined distance of all the pumpkins chunked at the 2005 championship totaled almost 10 miles (16 km). Each year the festival raises about $100,000 and benefits St. Jude Children's Hospital.

The United States'
LARGEST PUMPKIN-THROWING CONTESTS
Spectators

Millsboro, Delaware	Busit, New York	Morton, Illinois	York, Pennsylvania	Salina, Kansas
30,000	5,000	3,500	3,000	1,200

State with the
Most Lightning Strikes

Florida

The United States'
MOST LIGHTNING STRIKES

Annual bolts per square mile (2.6 sq. km.)

Florida	Louisiana	Mississippi	Texas	Arizona
25.1	17.1	15.5	15.0	13.9

Southern Florida is known as the Lightning Capital of the United States, with 59 bolts occurring over each square mile (2.6 sq km)—the equivalent of 10 city blocks—each year. Some 70% of all strikes occur between noon and 6:00 P.M., and the most dangerous months are July and August. Most lightning bolts measure 2 to 3 miles (5.2 to 7.8 km) long and can generate between 100 million to 1 billion volts of electricity. The air in a lightning bolt is heated to 50,000 degrees Fahrenheit (27,760 degrees C).

State with the Largest
State Sports Hall of Fame

Georgia

The United States'
LARGEST SPORTS HALLS OF FAME

Square feet/square meters

Georgia Sports Hall of Fame	Alabama Sports Hall of Fame	Virgina Sports Hall of Fame	Mississippi Sports Hall of Fame	Kansas Sports Hall of Fame
43,000 sq. ft. 3,995 sq. m.	33,000 sq. ft. 3,066 sq. m.	32,000 sq. ft. 3,000 sq. m.	21,542 sq. ft. 2,001 sq. m.	20,000 sq. ft. 1,900 sq. m.

The Georgia Sports Hall of Fame fills 43,000 square feet (3,995 sq m) with memorabilia from Georgia's most accomplished prep, college, amateur, and professional athletes. Some 230,000 bricks, 245 tons (222 t.) of steel, and 7,591 pounds (3,443 kg.) of glass were used in its construction. The hall owns more than 3,000 artifacts and displays about 1,000 of them at a time. Some Hall of Famers include baseball legend Hank Aaron, Olympic basketball great Theresa Edwards, and Super Bowl I champion Bill Curry.

State with the Largest Submillimeter Wavelength Telescope

Hawaii

Mount Kea—located in the island of Hawaii—is the home to the world's largest submillimeter telescope with a diameter of 49 feet (15 m). The James Clerk Maxwell Telescope (JCMT) is used to study our solar system, interstellar dust and gas, and distant galaxies. Mount Kea also houses the world's largest optical/infrared (Keck I and II) and dedicated infrared (UKIRT) telescopes in the world. Mount Kea is an ideal spot for astronomy because the atmosphere above the dormant volcano is very dry with little cloud cover, and its distance from city lights ensures a dark night sky.

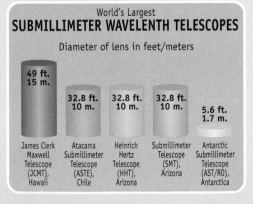

World's Largest
SUBMILLIMETER WAVELENTH TELESCOPES

Diameter of lens in feet/meters

James Clerk Maxwell Telescope (JCMT), Hawaii	Atacama Submillimeter Telescope (ASTE), Chile	Heinrich Hertz Telescope (HHT), Arizona	Submillimeter Telescope (SMT), Arizona	Antarctic Submillimeter Telescope (AST/RO), Antarctica
49 ft. 15 m.	32.8 ft. 10 m.	32.8 ft. 10 m.	32.8 ft. 10 m.	5.6 ft. 1.7 m.

State with the
Longest Main Street

Idaho

The city of Island Park, Idaho, has the country's longest main street at 33 miles (53.1 km). In the 1930s, the stretch of land ran through the city and housed several casinos that employed many residents. Laws stated that gambling could not take place outside city lines, so a businessman decided to make the entire strip of land a part of the town. The town, however, only measures about 500 feet (152.4 m) wide in some sections. Known as U.S. 20, the road is the main highway into Yellowstone National Park.

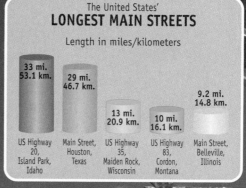

The United States'
LONGEST MAIN STREETS
Length in miles/kilometers

US Highway 20, Island Park, Idaho	Main Street, Houston, Texas	US Highway 35, Maiden Rock, Wisconsin	US Highway 83, Cordon, Montana	Main Street, Belleville, Illinois
33 mi. 53.1 km.	29 mi. 46.7 km.	13 mi. 20.9 km.	10 mi. 16.1 km.	9.2 mi. 14.8 km.

State with the
Largest Cookie Factory

Illinois

The Nabisco factory covers 46 acres (18.6 ha) on South Kedzie Avenue in Chicago, Illinois. The 1.75 million-square-foot (162,000-sq-m) cookie factory is also one of the largest bakeries in the world. The Nabisco plant employs about 2,000 workers, and they produce about 320 million pounds (145 million kg) of Oreo cookies, Fig Newtons, and Ritz Crackers each year. The factory has storage capacity of 8.5 million pounds (3.9 million kg) of flour, 2.4 million pounds (1.1 million kg) of sugar, and 1.5 million pounds (680,388 kg) of vegetable oil. There are also 20 ovens in the facility that measure about 300 feet (91 m) in length.

The United States'
LARGEST COOKIE FACTORIES

Area in square feet/square meters

Nabisco, Illinois	Entemann's, New York	Interstate Bakeries Corporation, Missouri	Pepperidge Farm, Connecticut	Otis Spunkmeyer, Texas
1.75 M sq. ft. 162,000 sq. m.	500,000 sq. ft. 46,452 sq. m.	325,000 sq. ft. 30,194 sq. m.	265,000 sq. ft. 24,619 sq. m.	97,000 sq. ft. 9,012 sq. m.

State with the Largest
Half Marathon

Indiana

Cars aren't the only things racing in Indianapolis. Each May some 35,000 runners take part in the Indianapolis Life 500 Festival Mini-Marathon. This makes the mini-marathon the nation's largest half marathon and the nation's eighth longest road race. The 13.1-mile (21.1-km) race winds through downtown and includes a lap along the Indianapolis Motor Speedway oval. About 100 musical groups entertain the runners as they complete the course. A giant pasta dinner and after-race party await the runners at the end of the day. The mini-marathon is part of a weekend celebration that centers around the Indianapolis 500 auto race.

The United States'
LARGEST HALF MARATHONS

Number of runners

Indianapolis Life 500 Festival Mini-Marathon, Indiana	County Race for the Cure, Michigan	Boston Athletic Association Half Marathon, Massachusetts	Rock 'n' Roll Half Marathon, Arizona	Chicago Half Marathon, Illinois
35,000	25,000	20,000	20,000	18,000

State with the
Highest Egg Production

Iowa

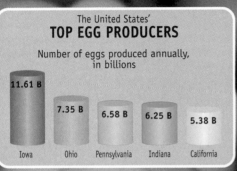

The United States'
TOP EGG PRODUCERS

Number of eggs produced annually,
in billions

11.61 B — Iowa
7.35 B — Ohio
6.58 B — Pennsylvania
6.25 B — Indiana
5.38 B — California

Iowa tops all other states in the country in egg production, turning out 11.6 billion eggs per year. That's enough to give every person in the United States more than 3 dozen eggs each! That's a good thing, because each person in America eats about 256 eggs per year. The state has 42 million laying hens, and each is capable of laying about 240 eggs a year. These hungry hens eat about 40 million bushels of corn and 20 million bushels of soybeans annually. In addition to selling the eggs as is, Iowa's processing plants turn them into frozen, liquid, dried, or specialty egg products.

State with the
Windiest City

Kansas

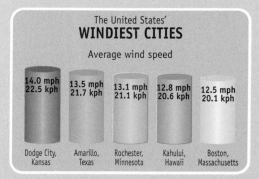

The United States'
WINDIEST CITIES

Average wind speed

14.0 mph 22.5 kph	13.5 mph 21.7 kph	13.1 mph 21.1 kph	12.8 mph 20.6 kph	12.5 mph 20.1 kph
Dodge City, Kansas	Amarillo, Texas	Rochester, Minnesota	Kahului, Hawaii	Boston, Massachusetts

According to average annual wind speeds collected by the National Climatic Data Center, Dodge City is the windiest city in the United States, with an average wind speed of 14 miles (22.5 km) per hour. Located in Ford County, the city boarders the Santa Fe Trail and is rich in history. The city was established in 1872 and had a reputation as a tough cowboy town. With help from legendary sheriffs like Wyatt Earp, order was restored and the town grew steadily. Today tourists come to take in the area history.

261

State with the
Largest Fireworks Display

Kentucky

The World's
LARGEST FIREWORKS DISPLAYS

Number of fireworks shells used

56,000	35,000	22,000	12,000	10,000
Thunder Over Louisville, Kentucky	Macy's 4th of July, New York	Sailfest, Connecticut	Pops Concert at the Esplanade, Massachusetts	Central Pennsylvania 4th Fest, Pennsylvania

Thunder Over Louisville is the world's largest fireworks display, drawing approximately 500,000 spectators each year. It is the opening ceremony for the Kentucky Derby Festival. Eight 400-foot (122-m) barges line both sides of the Second Street Bridge and serve as a stage for the 28-minute show. During the show, some 60 tons (54 t) of fireworks shells and 250 tons (227 t) of launching tubes are used. The show is set to all types of music, ranging from rock and roll to Broadway tunes. Millions of people worldwide also see the show when it's rebroadcast on the 4th of July to 150 countries.

State with the
Largest Alligator Population

Louisiana

GATOR XING
NEXT 1/2 MILE

There are approximately 2 million alligators living in Louisiana. That's equal to the number of people living in Houston, Texas—the nation's fourth-largest city! In 1986, Louisiana began an alligator ranching business, which encouraged farmers to raise thousands of the reptiles each year. The farmers must return some alligators to the wild, but they are allowed to sell the rest for profit. And, the released alligators have an excellent chance of thriving in the wild because they have been well fed and are a good size. Although alligators can be found in the state's bayous, swamps, and ponds, most live in Louisiana's 3 million acres (1.2 million ha) of coastal marshland.

The United States'
LARGEST ALLIGATOR POPULATIONS

Total number of alligators, in millions/thousands

Louisiana	Florida	Texas	South Carolina	Georgia
2.0 M	1.6 M	220,000	100,000	80,000

State with the
Oldest State Fair

Maine

The first Skowhegan State Fair took place in 1819—a year before Maine officially became a state! The fair took place in January, and hundreds of people came despite the harsh weather. Originally sponsored by the Somerset Central Agricultural Society, the fair name became official in 1842. State fairs were very important in the early 1900s. With no agricultural colleges in existence, fairs became the best way for farmers to learn about new agricultural methods and equipment. Today the Skowhegan State Fair features more than 7,000 exhibitors who compete for prize money totaling more than $200,000. The fair also includes a demolition derby, a children's barnyard, concerts, livestock exhibits, and arts and crafts.

The United States'
OLDEST STATE FAIRS
Year fair first held

1819	1820	1851	1851	1862
Skowhegan State Fair, Maine	Three County Fair, Maine	Bangor State Fair, Maine	Brooklyn Fair, Connecticut	Woodstock Fair, Vermont

State with the Oldest Airport

Maryland

Wright brothers exhibit at
The College Park Aviation Museum

The United States' OLDEST AIRPORTS

Year opened

1909	1911	1920	1921	1924
College Park Airport, Maryland	Roberston Airport, Connecticut	Hartness State Airport, Vermont	Bell County Airport, Kentucky	Page Field, Florida

The Wright brothers founded College Park Airport in 1909 to teach Army officers how to fly and it has been in operation ever since. The airport is now owned by the Maryland-National Capital Park and Planning Commission and is on the Register of Historic Places. Many aviation "firsts" occurred at this airport, such as the first woman passenger in the United States (1909), the first test of a bomb-dropping device (1911), and the first U.S. Air Mail Service (1918). The College Park Aviation Museum is located on the grounds and houses aviation memorabilia.

State with the
Oldest Baseball Stadium

Massachusetts

Fenway Park opened its doors to baseball fans on April 20, 1912. The Boston Red Sox—the park's home team—won the World Series that year. The park celebrated in 2004 when the Sox won the World Series again. The park is also the home of the Green Monster—a giant 37-foot (11.3-m) wall with an additional 23-foot (7-m) screen that has plagued home-run hitters since the park first opened. The park's unique dimensions were not to prevent home-runs, however. They were meant to keep nonpaying fans outside. A seat out in the right-field bleachers is painted red to mark where the longest measurable home-run hit inside the park landed. It measured 502 feet (153 m) and was hit by Ted Williams in 1946. Some of the other baseball legends who played at Fenway include Cy Young, Babe Ruth, Jimmie Fox, and Carlton Fisk.

The United States'
OLDEST BASEBALL STADIUMS
Year built

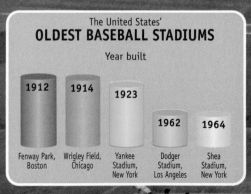

1912	1914	1923	1962	1964
Fenway Park, Boston	Wrigley Field, Chicago	Yankee Stadium, New York	Dodger Stadium, Los Angeles	Shea Stadium, New York

BOSTON RED SOX

State with the World's
Largest Indoor Waterfall

Michigan

The 114-foot (34.7-m) waterfall located in the lobby of the International Center in Detroit, Michigan, is the tallest indoor waterfall in the world. The backdrop of this impressive waterfall is a 9,000-square-foot (840-sq-m) slab of marble that was imported from the Greek island of Tinos and installed by eight marble craftsmen. About 6,000 gallons (27,276 l) of water spill down the waterfall each minute. That's the liquid equivalent of 80,000 cans of soda! Visitors can see this $1.5 million creation as they stroll through the International Center, which also houses many retail shops. Located in the historic Trappers Alley in the Greektown section of the city, the 8-story building was formerly used as a seed warehouse.

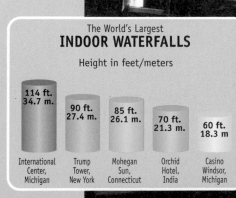

The World's Largest
INDOOR WATERFALLS

Height in feet/meters

114 ft. 34.7 m.	90 ft. 27.4 m.	85 ft. 26.1 m.	70 ft. 21.3 m.	60 ft. 18.3 m
International Center, Michigan	Trump Tower, New York	Mohegan Sun, Connecticut	Orchid Hotel, India	Casino Windsor, Michigan

State with the
Largest Indoor Theme Park

Minnesota

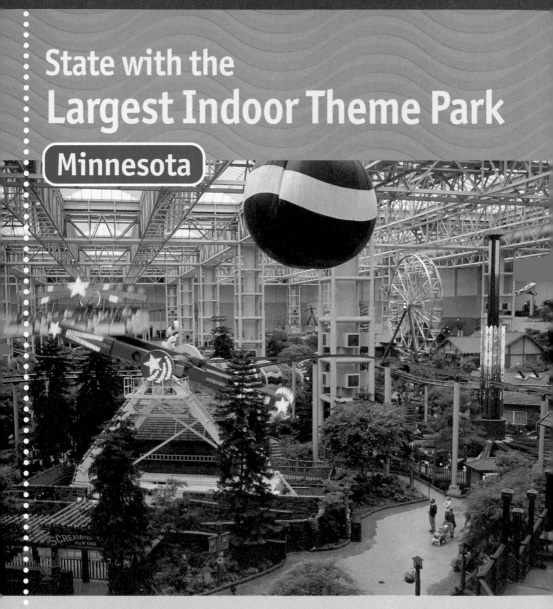

The Park at MOA is located inside of the Mall of America and covers 7 acres (2.8 ha). The park offers 30 rides, including the Xcel Energy Log Chute, skyscraper Ferris wheel, Timber Twister roller coaster, Mighty Axe, and the Mystery Mine Ride. Some of the other attractions at the park are a rock-climbing wall, petting zoo, and game arcade. The park is completely heated by a giant glass ceiling and the guests' body heat. Even during the cold Minnesota winter, the air conditioning is running full time.

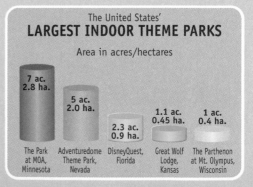

The United States'
LARGEST INDOOR THEME PARKS

Area in acres/hectares

7 ac. 2.8 ha.	5 ac. 2.0 ha.	2.3 ac. 0.9 ha.	1.1 ac. 0.45 ha.	1 ac. 0.4 ha.
The Park at MOA, Minnesota	Adventuredome Theme Park, Nevada	DisneyQuest, Florida	Great Wolf Lodge, Kansas	The Parthenon at Mt. Olympus, Wisconsin

State with the Most Catfish

Mississippi

There are more than 541 million catfish in Mississippi—more than 72% of the world's farm-raised supply. That's almost enough to give every person in the state 235 fish each. Mississippi's catfish crop is worth about $245 million annually. There are about 400 catfish producers farming 103,000 water acres (41,680 ha). The state's residents are quite proud of their successful fish industry and celebrate at the World Catfish Festival in Belzoni.

The States with the
MOST CATFISH

Number of catfish, in millions

Mississippi	Louisiana	Alabama	Arkansas	Texas
541.6 M	213.7 M	188.2 M	119.8 M	72.4 M

State with the Largest Outdoor Musical Theater

Missouri

The United States' LARGEST OUTDOOR MUSICAL THEATERS

Square feet/square meters

The Muny, Missouri	80,000 sq. ft. / 7,432 sq. m.
Alpine Valley Music Theater, Wisconsin	55,000 sq. ft. / 5,100 sq. m.
Journal Pavilion, New Mexico	45,000 sq. ft. / 4,200 sq. m.
Miller Outdoor Theater, Texas	37,000 sq. ft. / 3,500 sq. m.
Starlight Theater, Missouri	12,000 sq. ft. / 1,100 sq. m.

The Municipal Theatre in St. Louis—affectionately known as The Muny—is the nation's largest outdoor theater, with 80,000 square feet (7,432 sq m) and 11,500 seats—about the same size as a regulation soccer field. Amazingly, construction on the giant theater was completed in just 42 days at a cost of $10,000. The theater opened in 1917 with a production of Verdi's *Aïda*, and the best seats cost only $1.00. Today, The Muny offers classic Broadway shows each summer, with past productions including *Aïda*, *The King and I*, *The Wizard of Oz*, and *Oliver!* And the last nine rows of the theater are always held as free seats for the public, just as they have been since The Muny opened.

State with the
Largest County Park

Montana

The United States'
LARGEST COUNTY PARKS

Size in acres/hectares

10,000 ac. 4,047 ha.	9,500 ac. 3,845 ha.	8,000 ac. 3,237 ha.	7,000 ac. 2,822 ha.	4,700 ac. 1,902 ha.
Beaver Creek Park, Montana	Grant Ranch County, California	Caspers Wilderness Park, California	Dorey Park, Virgina	Ward Pound Ridge Reservation, New York

Beaver Creek Park is the nation's largest county park with 10,000 acres (4,047 ha). Located at the base of the Bear Paw Mountains of Montana, the park measures about 1 mile (1.6 km) wide and 17 miles (27.3 km) long. Some of the most popular activities at the park include hiking, camping, cross-country skiing, and snowmobiling. Beaver Creek Park also has two large lakes that are stocked with trout for year-round fishing. Many animals also call the park home, including mule deer, bobcat, beaver, coyote, fox, mink, pheasants, grouse, Golden Eagles, and hawks.

State with the Largest Nocturnal Animal Exhibit

Nebraska

The Henry Doorly Zoo in Omaha, Nebraska, is home to the Kingdom of the Night exhibit, which occupies more than 42,000 square feet (3,901 sq m) of the zoo's Desert Dome. There are five different areas inside the 0.75 acre (0.3 ha) exhibit, including the canyon, the African diorama, the wet cave, the Eucalyptus forest, and the dry cave. Some of the animals featured in Kingdom of the Night include aardvarks, meerkats, Japanese giant salamander, wallabies, and bats. The zoo has reversed the daily cycle of these animals, making the exhibit light in the night and dark in the day, so the animals are most active when visitors are there.

The United States'
LARGEST NOCTURNAL ANIMAL EXHIBITS

Size in square feet/square meters

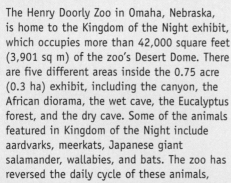

Kingdoms of the Night, Nebraska	Animals of the Night, Tennessee	Day and Night Exhibit, Washington	Masters of the Night, Texas	Frogtown USA, OH
42,000 sq. ft. 3,901 sq. m.	35,000 sq. ft. 3,252 sq. m.	20,000 sq. ft. 1,858 sq. m.	5,000 sq. ft. 465 sq. m.	600 sq. ft. 56 sq. m.

State with the World's
Largest Glass Sculpture

Nevada

The World's
LARGEST GLASS SCULPTURES

Length in feet/meters

Fiori di Como, Nevada	The Chihuly Tower, Oklahoma	Borealis, Michigan	Cobalt Blue Chandelier, Washington	Crystal Gate, Bahamas
65.7 ft. 20 m.	55 ft. 16 m.	49.2 ft. 15 m.	29 ft. 8.8 m.	18 ft. 5.5 m.

Fiori di Como—the breathtaking chandelier at the Bellagio Hotel in Las Vegas, Nevada—measures 65.7 feet by 29.5 feet (20 m by 9 m). Created by Dale Chihuly, the handblown glass chandelier consists of more than 2,000 discs of colored glass. Each disc is about 18 inches (45.7 cm) wide and hangs about 20 feet (6.1 m) overhead. Together, these colorful discs look like a giant field of flowers. The chandelier required about 10,000 pounds of steel (4,540 kg) and 40,000 pounds (18,160 kg) of handblown glass. The sculpture's name translates to "Flowers of Como." The Bellagio was modeled after the hotel on Lake Como in Italy.

273

State with the
Oldest Post Office

The Hinsdale Post Office opened its doors in 1816, and has been in operation ever since. At that time, James Madison was the country's fourth president and the Civil War was still 45 years away. The mail was delivered by horse and wagon and there were no paved roads. In the mid 1800s, nearby Brattleboro, Vermont, was connected to the railroad and mail was moved that way. In 1905, the first rural route was in place and mail was delivered to some homes by horse and buggy. Today the historic building is equipped with modern technology, and the price of a stamp is 3100% higher than it was in 1816.

New Hampshire

The United States'
OLDEST POST OFFICES

Year established

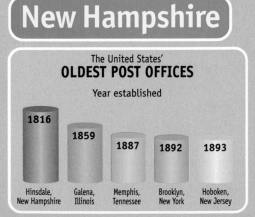

1816	1859	1887	1892	1893
Hinsdale, New Hampshire	Galena, Illinois	Memphis, Tennessee	Brooklyn, New York	Hoboken, New Jersey

State with the World's
Longest Boardwalk

New Jersey

The World's
LONGEST BOARDWALKS

Length in miles/kilometers

4.0 mi. 6.4 km.	3.0 mi. 4.8 km.	2.5 mi. 4.0 km.	2.3 mi. 3.7 km.	2.0 mi. 3.2 km.
Atlantic City, New Jersey	Coney Island, New York	FDR Boardwalk, New York	Corkscrew Swamp Sanctuary, Florida	Jarzoo Boardwalk, Sweden

The famous boardwalk in Atlantic City, New Jersey, stretches for 4 miles (6.4 km) along the beach. Combined with the adjoining boardwalk in Ventnor, the length increases to just under 6 miles (9.7 km). The 60-foot-(18-m) wide boardwalk opened on June 26, 1870. It was the first boardwalk built in the United States, and was designed to keep sand out of the tourists' shoes. Today the boardwalk is filled with amusement parks, shops, restaurants, and hotels. About 37 million people take a stroll along the walk each year, and many of them sample the city's famous salt-water taffy and fresh-roasted peanuts.

State with the World's
Largest Balloon Festival

New Mexico

During the 2006 Kodak Albuquerque International Balloon Fiesta, approximately 700 hot air and gas-filled balloons sailed across the sky. Held each October, the Fiesta draws hundreds of thousands of spectators. This event attracts balloons from around the world, and is often seen in more than 50 countries. The festival takes place in the 350-acre (142-ha) Balloon Fiesta State Park. The Balloon Fiesta has also hosted some prestigious balloon races, including the Gordon Bennett Cup (1993), World Gas Balloon Championship (1994), and the America's Challenge Gas Balloon Race (1995).

The World's
LARGEST BALLOON FESTIVALS

Approximate number of balloons

Albuquerque, New Mexico	Gallup, New Mexico	Greenville, South Carolina	Gatineau, Canada	Scottsdale, Arizona
700	200	150	150	150

State with the
Largest Underwater Tunnel

New York

The Brooklyn-Battery Tunnel measures 1.73 miles (2.78 km) long, making it the longest underwater tunnel in North America and longest continuous underwater vehicular tunnel in the world. The tunnel passes under the East River and connects Battery Park in Manhattan with the Red Hook section of Brooklyn. It took 13,900 tons (12,609 t) of steel, about 205,000 cubic yards (156,700 cu m) of concrete, approximately 1,871 miles (3,011 km) of electrical wire, some 883,391 bolts, and 799,000 wall and ceiling tiles to build the tunnel. Completed in 1950, the $90-million tunnel carries about 60,000 vehicles a day.

The United States'
LONGEST UNDERWATER TUNNELS
Length in miles/kilometers

1.73 mi. 2.78 km.	1.70 mi. 2.73 km.	1.69 mi. 2.72 km.	1.62 mi. 2.62 km.	1.56 mi. 2.51 km.
Brooklyn-Battery Tunnel, New York	E. Johnson Memorial Tunnel, Colorado	Eisenhower Memorial Tunnel, Colorado	Holland Tunnel, New York	Lincoln Tunnel, New York

State with the
Oldest State University

North Carolina

The University of North Carolina (UNC) was founded in 1789 but did not accept its first student at Chapel Hill until February 1795 because of a lack of funding. By the following month, the university consisted of two buildings, two professors, and 41 students. This makes UNC the only university in the United States to graduate students in the 18th century. Today, the University of North Carolina's 16 campuses have more than 28,000 undergraduates and 2,800 faculty. The university offers more than 100 fields of study, and grants bachelor's, master's, and doctoral degrees.

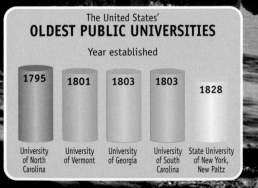

The United States'
OLDEST PUBLIC UNIVERSITIES

Year established

1795	1801	1803	1803	1828
University of North Carolina	University of Vermont	University of Georgia	University of South Carolina	State University of New York, New Paltz

State with the
Tallest Metal Sculptures

North Dakota

In August 2001, Gary Greff created a 110-foot- (33.5-m-) tall metal sculpture along the stretch of road between Gladstone and Regent, North Dakota. That's the height of an 11-story building! The 154-foot- (46.9-m-) long sculpture is called "Geese in Flight," and shows Canadian geese traveling across the prairie. Greff has created several other towering sculptures nearby, and the road has become known as the Enchanted Highway. He created these sculptures to attract tourists to the area and to support his hometown. He relies only on donations to finance his work.

The United States'
TALLEST METAL SCULPTURES
Height in feet/meters

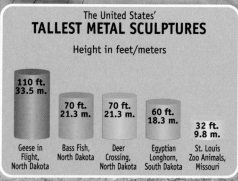

110 ft. 33.5 m.	70 ft. 21.3 m.	70 ft. 21.3 m.	60 ft. 18.3 m.	32 ft. 9.8 m.
Geese in Flight, North Dakota	Bass Fish, North Dakota	Deer Crossing, North Dakota	Egyptian Longhorn, South Dakota	St. Louis Zoo Animals, Missouri

State with the World's
Largest Twins Gathering

Ohio

The World's
LARGEST TWINS GATHERING

Number of attendees

Twins Day Festival, Ohio	Beijing Twins Festival, China	*"Deux et plus"* Gathering, France	International Twins Assoc. Annual Festival, Michigan	Annual Twins Gathering, New York
4,050	1,200	1,000	950	500

Each August, the town of Twinsburg, Ohio, hosts more than 4,000 twins at its annual Twins Day Festival. Both identical and fraternal twins from around the world participate, and many dress alike. The twins take part in games and contests, such as the oldest identical twins and the twins with the widest combined smile. There is also a "Double Take" parade, which is nationally televised. Since twins from ages 90 to just 11 days old have attended, there are special twin programs for all age groups. The event began in 1976 in honor of Aaron and Moses Wilcox, twin brothers who inspired the city to adopt its name in 1817.

State with the World's
Longest Multiple Arch Dam

Oklahoma

With a length of 6,565 feet (2,001 m), the Pensacola Dam is the world's longest multiple arch dam. Built in 1941, the dam is located on the Grand River and contains the Lake of the Cherokees—one of the largest reservoirs of the country with 46,500 surface acres (18,818 ha) of water. The dam stands 145 feet (44 m) high. It was made out of 535,000 cubic yards of concrete, some 655,000 barrels of cement, another 10 million pounds (4.5 million kg) of structural steel, and 75,000 pounds (340,194 kg) of copper. The dam cost $27 million to complete.

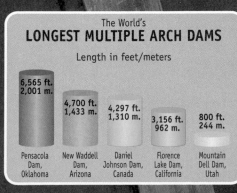

The World's
LONGEST MULTIPLE ARCH DAMS

Length in feet/meters

6,565 ft. 2,001 m.	4,700 ft. 1,433 m.	4,297 ft. 1,310 m.	3,156 ft. 962 m.	800 ft. 244 m.
Pensacola Dam, Oklahoma	New Waddell Dam, Arizona	Daniel Johnson Dam, Canada	Florence Lake Dam, California	Mountain Dell Dam, Utah

State with the
Deepest Lake

The United States'
DEEPEST LAKES
Greatest depth in feet/meters

Crater Lake, Oregon	Lake Tahoe, California/ Nevada	Lake Chelan, Washington	Lake Superior, Michigan/ Minnesota/ Wisconsin	Lake Pend Oreille, Idaho
1,932 ft. 589 m.	1,643 ft. 501 m.	1,604 ft. 489 m.	1,330 ft. 405 m.	1,171 ft. 357 m.

At a depth of 1,932 feet (589 m), Crater Lake in Southern Oregon partially fills the remains of an old volcano basin. The crater was formed almost 7,700 years ago when Mount Mazama erupted, and then collapsed. The lake averages about 5 miles (8 km) in diameter. Crater Lake National Park—the nation's fifth oldest park—surrounds the majestic lake and measures 249 square miles (645 sq km). The area's large snowfalls average 530 inches (1,346 cm) a year, and supply Crater Lake with its water. In additional to being the United States' deepest lake, it's also the eighth deepest lake in the world.

State with the
Oldest Drive-In Theater

Pennsylvania

Shankweiler's Drive-In Theater opened in 1934 and is the country's second drive-in theater, but it is the oldest one still operating today. Located in Orefield, Pennsylvania, the single-screen theater can accommodate 320 cars. Approximately 90% of the theater's guests are children. Although they originally used sound boxes located beside the cars, today patrons can tune into a special radio station to hear the movies' music and dialogue. Shankweiler's is open from April to September.

The United States'
OLDEST DRIVE-IN THEATERS
Year opened

1934	1937	1939	1943	1946
Shankweiler's Drive-In Theater, Pennsylvania	Lynn Auto Theatre, Ohio	Saco Drive-In, Maine	Sunset Drive-In Theater, Pennsylvania	Hiway 50 Drive-In Theater, Tennessee

State with the
Oldest Temple

Rhode Island

The Touro Synagogue was dedicated during Hanukkah in December 1763 and is the oldest temple in the United States. Located in Newport, Rhode Island, the temple was designed by famous architect Peter Harrison and took four years to complete. In addition to serving as a symbol of religious freedom, the temple played another part in the country's history. When the British captured Newport in 1776, the temple briefly became a British hospital. Then, in 1781, George Washington met General Lafayette there to plan the final battles of the Revolution.

The United States'
OLDEST TEMPLES

Year opened

1763	1824	1825	1849	1886
Touro Synagogue, Rhode Island	Kahal Kadosh Beth Elohim Synagogue, South Carolina	B'nai Jeshurun, New York	Shul of New York, New York	Oheve Sholom Talmud Torah, District of Columbia

State with the
Oldest Landscaped Gardens

South Carolina

The geometrical garden patterns in Middleton Place Gardens were designed by Henry Middleton in 1741 and were modeled after the gardens at the Palace of Versailles in France. They were first opened to the public in the 1920s. Today, the gardens on this 65-acre (26.3 ha) Charleston plantation are laid out in almost the same fashion as when they were planted more than 250 years ago. Some of the plants that are featured at Middleton Place Gardens include camellias, daffodils, magnolias, jasmine, columbine, and hydrangea. The House Museum is also located on the grounds and displays some of the Middleton family's furniture, art, and documents.

The United States'
OLDEST LANDSCAPED GARDENS

Year established

1741	1853	1891	1907	1932
Middleton Place Gardens, South Carolina	Missouri Botanical Gardens, Missouri	New York Botanical Gardens, New York	Longwood Gardens, Pennsylvania	Hershey Gardens, Pennsylvania

State with the Largest
Petrified Wood Collection

South Dakota

Lemmon's Petrified Wood Park in South Dakota is home to 30 acres (12.1 ha) of petrified wood. It covers an entire city block in downtown Lemmon. It was built between 1930 and 1932 when locals collected petrified wood from the area and constructed displays. One structure in the park known as The Castle weighs more than 300 pounds (136 kg) and is made partly from petrified wood and partly of petrified dinosaur and mammoth bones. Other exhibits include a wishing well, a waterfall, the Lemmon Pioneer Museum, and hundreds of pile sculptures.

The United States'
LARGEST PETRIFIED WOOD COLLECTIONS

Area in acres/hectares

30 ac. 12.1 ha.	27 ac. 10.9 ha.	24 ac. 9.7 ha.	20 ac. 8.1 ha.	18 ac. 7.3 ha.
Lemmon's Petrified Wood Park, South Dakota	Long Logs Forest, Arizona	Rainbow Forest, Arizona	Crystal Forest, Arizona	Black Forest, Arizona

State with the World's
Largest Freshwater Aquarium

Tennessee

The Tennessee Aquarium in Chattanooga is an impressive 130,000 square feet (12,077 sq m), making it the largest freshwater aquarium in the world. In addition, the aquarium features a 60,000-square-foot (5,574-sq-m) building dedicated to the ocean and the creatures that live there. Permanent features in the aquarium include Discovery Hall, and an Environmental Learning Lab. Some of the aquarium's 12,000 animals include baby alligators, paddlefish, lake sturgeon, seadragons, and pipefish. And to feed all of these creatures, the aquarium goes through 12,000 crickets, 33,300 worms, and 1,200 pounds (545 kg) of seafood each month!

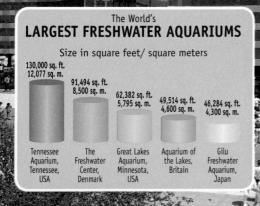

The World's
LARGEST FRESHWATER AQUARIUMS

Size in square feet/ square meters

130,000 sq. ft.
12,077 sq. m.

91,494 sq. ft.
8,500 sq. m.

62,382 sq. ft.
5,795 sq. m.

49,514 sq. ft.
4,600 sq. m.

46,284 sq. ft.
4,300 sq. m.

Tennessee Aquarium, Tennessee, USA

The Freshwater Center, Denmark

Great Lakes Aquarium, Minnesota, USA

Aquarium of the Lakes, Britain

Gilu Freshwater Aquarium, Japan

287

State with the
Biggest Ferris Wheel

Texas

The State Fair of Texas boasts the nation's largest Ferris wheel. Called the Texas Star, this colossal wheel measures 212 feet (64.6 m) high. That's taller than a 20-story building! The Texas Star was built in Italy and shipped to Texas for its debut at the 1986 fair. Located in the 277-acre (112 ha) Fair Park, the Texas Star is just one of the 70 rides featured at the fair. The three-week-long State Fair of Texas is the biggest state fair in the country and brings in about $350 million in revenues annually. It is held in the fall, and the giant Ferris wheel is not the only grand-scale item there. Big Tex, a 52-foot- (15.9-m-) tall cowboy, is the fair's mascot and the biggest cowboy in the United States.

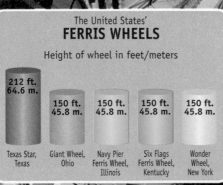

The United States'
FERRIS WHEELS

Height of wheel in feet/meters

212 ft. 64.6 m.	150 ft. 45.8 m.	150 ft. 45.8 m.	150 ft. 45.8 m.	150 ft. 45.8 m.
Texas Star, Texas	Giant Wheel, Ohio	Navy Pier Ferris Wheel, Illinois	Six Flags Ferris Wheel, Kentucky	Wonder Wheel, New York

State with the World's
Largest Human-Made Hole

Utah

Bingham Canyon—a working mine in the Oquirrh Mountains—is the largest human-made hole in the world. It measures 2.5 miles (4 km) wide and 0.5 miles (0.8 km) deep. It is so large that astronauts can even see it from space. Miners first began digging in the area in 1903. Today approximately 63 million tons (57 million t) of ore and 123 million tons (112 million t) of waste are removed from the canyon each year. Bingham Canyon is one of the largest copper mining operations in the world. It has produced more than 15 million tons (13.6 million t) of copper in the last 100 years. Silver and gold are also mined there.

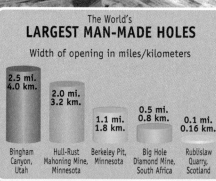

The World's
LARGEST MAN-MADE HOLES

Width of opening in miles/kilometers

2.5 mi.
4.0 km.

2.0 mi.
3.2 km.

1.1 mi.
1.8 km.

0.5 mi.
0.8 km.

0.1 mi.
0.16 km.

Bingham
Canyon,
Utah

Hull-Rust
Mahoning Mine,
Minnesota

Berkeley Pit,
Minnesota

Big Hole
Diamond Mine,
South Africa

Rublislaw
Quarry,
Scotland

State that Produces the Most Maple Syrup

Vermont

Maple syrup production in Vermont totaled 410,000 gallons (1,552,000 l) in 2005 and accounted for about 33% of the United States' total yield that year. There are about 2,000 maple syrup producers with 2.14 million tree taps in Vermont, and the annual production generates more than $13.7 million. It takes about five tree taps to collect enough maple sap—approximately 40 gallons (150 l)—to produce just 1 gallon (3.79 l) of syrup. Vermont maple syrup is also made into maple sugar, maple cream, and maple candies.

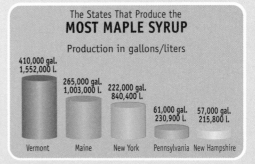

The States That Produce the
MOST MAPLE SYRUP

Production in gallons/liters

410,000 gal.
1,552,000 l.

265,000 gal.
1,003,000 l.

222,000 gal.
840,400 l.

61,000 gal.
230,900 l.

57,000 gal.
215,800 l.

Vermont   Maine   New York   Pennsylvania   New Hampshire

State with the
Largest Office Building

Virginia

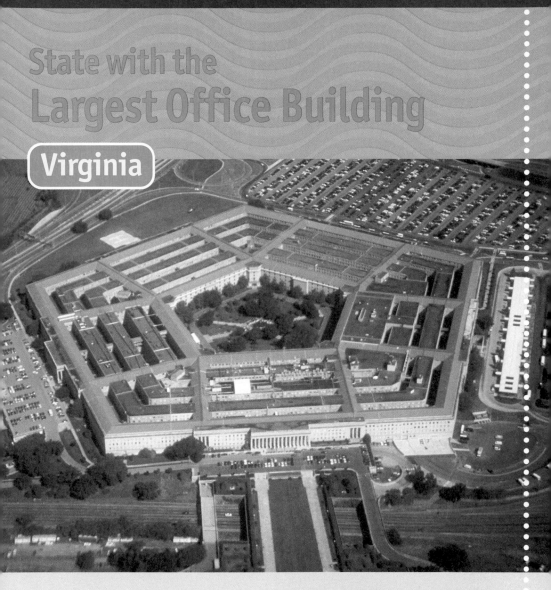

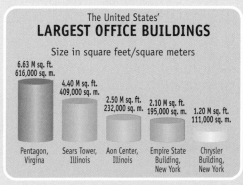

The United States'
LARGEST OFFICE BUILDINGS

Size in square feet/square meters

6.63 M sq. ft.
616,000 sq. m.

4.40 M sq. ft.
409,000 sq. m.

2.50 M sq. ft.
232,000 sq. m.

2.10 M sq. ft.
195,000 sq. m.

1.20 M sq. ft.
111,000 sq. m.

Pentagon, Virgina | Sears Tower, Illinois | Aon Center, Illinois | Empire State Building, New York | Chrysler Building, New York

The Pentagon Building in Arlington, Virginia, measures 6,636,360 square feet (616,538 sq m) and covers 583 acres (236 ha). In fact, the National Capitol can fit inside the building five times! Although the Pentagon contains 17.5 miles (28.2 km) of hallways, the design of the building allows people to reach any destination in about 7 minutes. The Pentagon is almost like a small city, employing about 25,000 people. About 200,000 phone calls are made there daily, and the internal post office handles about 1.2 million pieces of mail each month.

State with the
Longest Train Tunnel

Washington

CASCADE TUNNEL
7.8 MILES LONG   ELEVATION 2,247 FEET
41,152 FEET LONG   COMPLETED 1928

The United States'
LONGEST TRAIN TUNNELS

Length miles/kilometers

7.79 mi. 12.6 km.	7.78 mi. 12.5 km.	6.21 mi. 10.0 km.	4.70 mi. 7.56 km.	3.60 mi. 5.79 km.
Cascade Tunnel, Washington	Flathead Tunnel, Missouri	Moffat Tunnel, Colorado	Hoosac Tunnel, Massachusetts	BART Transbay Tube, California

The Cascade Tunnel runs through the Cascade Mountains in central Washington and measures almost 7.8 miles (12.6 km) long. The tunnel connects the towns of Berne and Scenic. It was built by the Great Northern Railway in 1929 to replace the original tunnel that was built at an elevation frequently hit with snow slides. To help cool the trains' diesel engines and remove fumes, the tunnel is equipped with huge fans that blow air during and after a train pass.

State with the Country's
Oldest Spa

West Virginia

GEORGE WASHINGTON'S
BATH TUB (1748)

The town of Bath in West Virginia is home to the country's first spa. In 1776, George Washington incorporated the town and named it Bath after the famous English town known for its Roman baths. Washington and his family relaxed in the healing waters, and eventually built a house nearby the increasingly popular health resort. Located in West Virginia's eastern panhandle, the Warm Spring Ridge produces about 2,000 gallons of water per minute at a temperature of 74°F. Today people come to Bath, which is also known as Berkeley Springs, for relaxation and health treatments.

The United States'
OLDEST SPAS

By year of incorporation

1776	1844	1854	1880	1909
Berkeley Springs, West Virginia	Warmer Springs Ranch, California	Vichy Hot Springs, California	Ojo Caliente, New Mexico	Steamboat Villa Hot Springs, Nevada

293

State with the Country's
Largest Water Park

Wisconsin

Noah's Ark in Wisconsin Dells sprawls for 70 acres (28.4 ha) and includes 36 waterslides. One of the most popular—Dark Voyage—takes visitors on a twisting rapids ride in the dark. The ride can pump 8,000 gallons (30,283 l) of water a minute. Visitors can also enjoy two wave pools, two mile-long "endless" rivers, and four children's play areas. It takes 5 million gallons (19 million l) of water—the equivalent of more than 14 Olympic swimming pools—to fill all the pools and operate the 3 miles (4.8 km) of waterslides. In 2005, the park's Black Anaconda ride opened. It's the country's longest watercoaster at 1/4 mile in length.

The United States'
LARGEST WATER PARKS

Size in acres/hectares

70 ac. 28.4 ha.	66 ac. 26.7 ha.	65 ac. 26.3 ha.	60 ac. 24.3 ha.	60 ac. 24.3 ha.
Noah's Ark, Wisconsin	Blizzard Beach, Florida	Schlitterbahn Beach Waterpark, Texas	Oceans of Fun, Missouri	Six Flags Splash Town, Texas

State with the
Largest Coal Mine

Wyoming

Black Thunder Mine is located near Wright, Wyoming, and produces about 100 million tons (90.7 million t) of coal each year. That's about 10% of the country's total production. The mine uses a giant earth-scraping machine that can extract about 3 tons (2.7 t) of coal per second! Miners fill about 25 miles (40 km) of coal cars each day. Black Thunder—which opened in 1977—has approximately 1 billion tons (907 million t) of coal still in the mine. Black Thunder is owned by Arch Coal—one of the world's largest coal producers—and employs about 600 people.

The United States'
LARGEST COAL MINES

Coal produced annually, in tons and metric tons

100 M tons 90.7 M t.	82 M tons 74.4 M t.	20 M tons 18.1 M t.	18 M tons 16.3 M t.	16 M tons 14.5 t.
Black Thunder, Wyoming	North Antelope Rochelle, Wyoming	MIBRAG, Missouri	Enlow Fork Mine, Pennsylvania	Freedom Mine, North Dakota

INDEX

A *Chorus Line*, 181
A Man for All Seasons, 180
Aaron, Hank, 23, 25, 27, 32, 33
Abdul-Jabbar, Kareem, 19
AC/DC, 175
Academy Awards®, 185
Acela Express, 238
Actors, 167, 168, 190
Actresses, 167, 169, 191
Adventure of the Seas, 240
Adventuredome Theme Park, 268
African elephant, 106, 110
Agassi, Andre, 45, 47
Agatston, Arthur, 193
Airports, 88, 89, 265
Akashi-Kaikyo, 84, 85
Akers, Thomas, 233
Alabama, 246, 269
Alaska, 146, 160, 161
Albatross, 98, 102
Albums, 171, 172, 175
Alexander, Shaun, 38
Allen, Marcus, 37
Alligators, 117, 119, 263
Al-Deayea, Mohamed, 58
Al-Talyania, Adnan Khamées, 58
Amarillo (TX), 261
Amazon River, 128, 129, 133
Amazon.com, 217
American Idol, 167
Amoco Cadiz, 163
Amphibians, 116
Amusement park, 79
Andersen, Morten, 39
Anderson, Gary, 39
Andes, 131

Andromeda Galaxy, 231
Animation, 183, 188
Anquetil, Jacques, 7
Anson, Cap, 33
Antarctic Submillimeter Telescope, 256
Aon Center, 291
Appalachian Mountains, 90
Arabian Desert, 127
Aragawa, 210
Arcain, Janeth, 18
Arctic Ocean, 130
Arctic tern, 100
Argentina, 59, 88
Arizona, 254
Arkansas, 269
Armstrong, Lance, 7
Arpège, 210
Artists, 194
Aswan, 149
Aswan High Dam, 149
Atacama Submillimeter Telescope, 256
Atlanta Braves, 251
Atlantic City, 275
Atlantic Empress, 163
Atlantic Ocean, 130, 134
Atlas Cheetah, 243
Australia, 81, 139, 143, 144, 186
Australian Desert, 127
Australian tiger beetle, 122
Austria, 144
Authors, 193
Automobiles, 239
Avocado, 159, 250
Awards, 179, 180, 185

Baffin Island, 132

Bailey, Donovan, 51
Baker, Buddy, 66
Bald eagle, 101
Balloon festivals, 276
Bangkok, 147
Bangladesh, 162
Banks, Ernie, 29
Baseball, 22–34, 251
Baseball stadiums, 266
Baseballs, 211
Basketball, 12–21
Bath (WV), 293
Bats, 111
Baylor, Elgin, 15
BD-5J Microjet, 242
Beatles, The, 175
Beaver Creek Park, 271
Becker, Boris, 45
Beckham, David, 60
Belgium, 140, 142
Bellagio Hotel, 273
Ben-Hur, 185
Berkeley Springs, 293
Berra, Yogi, 28
Bettencourt, Lilianne, 202
Bettis, Jerome, 36
Bigfoot 5, 241
Bigger Bang, The, 178
Bingham Canyon, 289
Bird, Sue, 18
Birds, 99–103
Black mamba, 114, 115
Black Thunder Mine, 295
Blanda, George, 39
Blossoms, 157
Blue Flame, 237
Blue Ridge Parkway, 90
Blue shark, 97, 104
Blue whale, 93, 105

BlueGene, 216
Blyleven, Bert, 24
Bobsled, 56
Bolivia, 133
Bonds, Barry, 22, 23, 26, 29, 211
Books, 193
Borg, Bjorn, 47
Borneo, 132, 157
Boston (MA), 266
Boston Celtics, 14
Boston Pops Concert at the Esplanade, 262
Bottled water, 140
Box office, 182, 183, 184, 192
Brady, Tom, 42
Brazil, 59, 73, 88, 133, 154
Bridges, 84, 85
Brin, Sergey, 206
Broadway, 180, 181
Brooklyn-Battery Tunnel, 277
Brooks & Dunn, 179
Brooks, Garth, 171, 179
Brown, Dan, 193
Brown, James, 176
Brown, Paul, 41
Browning, Kurt, 49
Bruce Almighty, 190
Bruckheimer, Jerry, 189
Bryant, Kobe, 17
Buffet, Warren, 203
Buffett, Jimmy, 173
Bugatti Veyron, 239
Buildings, 83
Burger King, 201
Burundi, 204
Busit (NY), 253
Butterflies, 121, 123

Cacti, 153
Caecilia Thompsoni, 116
California, 250, 260
California redwood, 155
Cameron, James, 192
Campanella, Roy, 29
Canada, 134, 141, 218
Carey, Mariah, 172
Carlton, Steve, 24, 31
Carpinchos, 107
Carrey, Jim, 190
Cars, 70, 73, 196, 212
Carter, Cris, 37

Cascade Tunnel, 292
Caspian Sea, 126
Castor bean plant, 158
Catchings, Tamika, 20
Catfish, 269
Cedar Point, 79, 252
Cell phones, 220, 221
Centaurus Galaxy, 231
Centenary, 135
CEOs, 197
Cereals, 198
Cerro El Condor, 125
Chamberlain, Wilt, 15, 19
Channel Tunnel, 74
Charles, Ray, 176
Charlie's Angels: Full Throttle, 191
Charon, 229
Chastain, Brandi, 61
Cheerios, 198
Cheetah, 109
Cherrapunji, 148
Chesney, Kenny, 173
Chicago, 80
Chicago Bears, 43
Chicago Bulls, 14
Chicago O'Hare Intl, 89
Chile, 160, 161
China, 73, 77, 87, 138, 154, 187, 215, 238
Chinese Giant Salamander, 116
Chocolate, 142, 200
Chrysler Building, 291
Chugach National Forest, 247
Clemens, Roger, 24, 26, 31
Cobb, Ty, 25, 27, 32
Coco de Mer, 159
Coconut crab, 92
College Park Airport, 265
Colorado, 84, 251
Colorado Rockies, 251
Columbia computer, 216
Commonwealth Bay, 150
Communication, 220, 221
Computers, 203, 214–218
Concerts, 178
Connecticut, 252
Constructions, 74–85
Cookie factories, 258
Cooper, Cynthia, 18, 20
Cope, Derrike, 66

Coropuna, 125
Country Music Awards, 179
Court Smith, Margaret, 46
Crater Lake, 282
Creamer, Paula, 8
Crops, 136, 137
Cross, Marcia, 169
Cruise ships, 240
Cruise, Tom, 182, 190
Crustaceans, 92
CSI: Crime Scene Investigation, 167
CSI: Miami, 167
Czech Republic, 220

Dallas Cowboys, 40
Dallol, 147
Daniel, Beth, 10
Da Vinci Code, The, 193
Dave Mathews Band, 178
Davenport, Lindsey, 44
Daytona 500, 66
De Bruijin, Inge, 53
Debundscha, 148
Del Piero, Alessandro, 60
Delaware, 253
Democratic Republic of Congo, 133
Denmark, 144, 218
Denver Nuggets, 16
Deserts, 127
Desperate Housewives, 167, 169
Detroit Pistons, 16
Diamond, Neil, 173
Diamonds, 135
Diaz, Cameron, 191
Dijkstra, Sjoukje, 48
DiMaggio, Joe, 28
Dion, Celine, 172, 174
Directors (movie), 189
Disasters, 160–165
Disneyland, 79
Dityatin, Aleksandr, 57
Dodger Stadium, 266
Donald, Luke, 9
Drive-in theaters, 283
Dunst, Kirsten, 184

Eagles, The, 175, 178
Earnhardt, Dale, 66
Earth, 225–227, 229, 232
Earthquakes, 161

East Timor, 204
eBay, 214, 217
Eggs, 102, 260
Egypt, 149, 222
El Guerrouj, Hicham, 6
El Paso, 248
Elliott, Bill, 66
Elway, John, 35
Emerson, Roy, 47
Empire State Building, 291
Erie Canal, 77
Erin Brockovich, 191
Ethiopia, 147, 204
Eureka Tower, 81
Evert-Lloyd, Chris, 46
Explorer of the Seas, 240

Fangs, 114
Fast food, 201
Faulk, Marshall, 37, 38
Favre, Brett, 35
Fawcett, Joy, 61
Fenway Park, 266
Ferdinand, Rio, 60
Ferris wheels, 288
Figini, Michela, 54
Fin whale, 93, 105
Final Fantasy: The Spirits Within, 188
Finland, 143
Finley, Michael, 17
Fiori di Como, 273
Fireworks, 262
Fish, 93–97
Fittipaldi, Emerson, 67
Fleming, Peggy, 48
Floods, 162
Florida, 246, 250, 254, 263
Flowers, 157
Football, 35–43
Ford, Harrison, 182
Foudy, Julie, 61
Fox, Jimmie, 28
Fox, Jorja, 169
Fox, Matthew, 168
France, 70, 87,140, 187, 199
Franchises, 201
Francis, Connie, 177
Franklin, Aretha, 177
Freedom of the Seas, 240
Freshwater aquariums, 287
Frogs, 112
Fruit, 136, 154

Furyk, Jim, 9

Gaboon viper, 114
Galápagos turtle, 117
Galaxies, 231, 234
Gandolfini, James, 168
Ganymede, 229
Gardens, 285
Garvey, Steve, 34
Gates, Bill, 203
Gateway National Recreation Area, 90
"Geese in flight," 279
Gehrig, Lou, 33, 34
Georgia, 255, 263
Georgia Sports Hall of Fame, 255
Germany, 59, 70, 142, 187, 199, 215, 219, 221
Germany II, 56
Giant flying fox, 111
Giant sequoia, 155
Giant spider crab, 92
Gibson, Mel, 189
Gill, Vince, 179
Giraffe, 106, 110
Glacier Bay National Park, 160
Glass sculptures, 273
Gobi Desert, 127
Golden Gate National Recreation Area, 90
Golden State Warriors, 14
Golf, 9–11
Goliath birdeater, 120
Google, 214
Gordon, Jeff, 68
Graf, Steffi, 44, 46
Grand Canal, 77
Gray whale, 105
Great Smokey Mountains, 90
Greece, 138
Green Bay Packers, 40
Green Day, 178
Green Monster, 266
Greenland, 132
Gretzky, Wayne, 63
Griffith-Joyner, Florence, 50
Gulbis, Natalie, 8

Hagen, Walter, 11
Halas, George, 41
Half marathons, 259

Hamilton, Scott, 49
Hamm, Mia, 61
Hanks, Tom, 182, 188
Hariri, Hind, 206
Harris Yamaha YLR500, 236
Harry Potter and the Chamber of Secrets, 183
Harry Potter and the Goblet of Fire, 183, 184
Harry Potter and the Prisoner of Azkaban, 184
Harry Potter and the Sorcerer's Stone, 183, 192
Hartsfield Atlanta Intl Airport, 89
Hassan, Hossam, 58
Hasselbeck, Matt, 42
Hatcher, Teri, 169
Hawaii, 250, 256
Hawk moth, 121
Heiss, Carol, 48
Helgenberger, Marg, 169
Hello Dolly, 180
Helms, Susan, 233
Henderson, Rickey, 27
Hershey's, 200
HersheyPark, 79
Hieb, Richard, 233
Himalayas, 124, 131
Hinault, Bernard, 7
Hingis, Martina, 44
Hinsdale Post Office, 274
Hockey, 62–65
Hogan, Ben, 11
Holdsclaw, Chamique, 20, 21
Holland Tunnel, 277
Holmes, Priest, 38
Home Depot, 249
Home runs, 22, 23
Honda Accord, 196
Honda CBR1100XX, 236
Honda Civic, 196
Hong Kong, 80, 86
Hotels, 207
Houston, Allan, 17
Houston, Whitney, 172
Huffman, Felicity, 169
Humber Estuary, 85
Hurricane Allen, 165
Hurricane Camille, 165
Hurricane Gilbert, 165
Hurricane Katrina, 165
Hurricane Mitch, 165

Hurricanes, 165

I, *Robot*, 190
Ice cream, 143
Iceland, 186, 205, 218, 220
Idaho, 257
Il Duomo, 82
Illinois, 258
India, 73, 148, 154, 187, 215
Indian Ocean, 130
Indiana, 260
Indianapolis 500, 67
Indianapolis Life 500 Festival
    Mini-Marathon, 259
Indonesia, 133, 134, 161,
    222
Indurain, Miguel, 7
Inkster, Juli, 10
Insects, 121–123
International Center, 267
International Space Station,
    233
Internet, 214, 215, 217, 218
Iowa, 260
Ireland, 139, 141, 142
Island Park, 257
Israel, 220
Italy, 59, 70, 87, 140, 219,
    220, 221
Iverson, Allen, 15
Izmit Bay, 85

Jackson, Alan, 179
Jackson, Lauren, 20
Jackson, Peter, 189
Jackson, Samuel L., 182
James Clerk Maxwell
    Telescope, 256
James, LeBron, 17
Jang, Jeong, 8
Japan, 70, 73, 74, 85, 134,
    161, 199, 210, 215, 219,
    221
Jarrett, Dale, 68
Jenkins, Hayes, 49
Jeter, Derek, 26
Jets, 242
Jin Mao Building, 83
Joel, Billy, 171
John, Elton, 171, 173, 176
Johnson, Abigail, 202
Johnson, Norm, 39
Johnson, Randy, 24, 31

Jones, Cobi, 58
Jones, Walter, 42
Jordan, Michael, 15, 19
Jupiter, 223, 225–230

Kafelnikov, Yevgeny, 45
Kalahari Desert, 127
Kamprad, Ingvar, 203
Kansas, 261
Kansas Sports Hall of Fame,
    255
Kentucky, 262
Kentucky Derby, 262
Kerr, Cristie, 8
Kingda Ka, 244
Kingdoms of the Night, 272
Kodak Albuquerque
    International Balloon
    Fiesta, 276
Koenigsegg CC85, 212, 239
Koenigsegg CCR, 212, 239
Komodo dragon, 117, 118
Koufax, Sandy, 31
Kwan, Michelle, 48

La Paz, 76
Lady Vols, 12
Laerdal Tunnel, 75
Lake Compounce, 252
Lakes, 126, 282
Lambeau, Curly, 41
Landry, Tom, 41
Large Magellanic Cloud, 231,
    234
Las Vegas, 207, 248
Last Emperor, The, 185
Last Samurai, The, 190
Laver, Rod, 47
Le Toiny, 207
Leaves, 152
Lebanon, 138
Led Zeppelin, 175
Lee, Brenda, 177
Lemmon's Petrified Wood
    Park, 286
Lendl, Ivan, 45
Leno, Jay, 170
Les Miserables, 181
Leslie, Lisa, 20, 21
Letterman, David, 170
Lhasa, 76
Lhotse, 124
Libya, 138

Light in the Piazza, The, 180
Lightning, 254
Lilly, Kristine, 61
Lituya bay, 160
Lizards, 118
Llullaillaco, 125
Lockheed SR-71 Blackbird,
    243
London, 71, 82, 86
London Underground, 71
*Lord of the Rings: The
    Return of the King*, 185,
    192
*Lord of the Rings: The Two
    Towers*, 192
Los Angeles Dodgers, 251
Los Angeles Intl., 89
Los Angeles Lakers, 14
Louisiana, 246, 254, 263,
    269
Lowery, Nick, 39
Lucas, George, 189
Luxembourg, 205, 220
Luyendyk, Arie, 67

Madagascar, 132
Maddux, Greg, 31
Madonna, 172, 174, 177
MagLev, 238
Maguire, Tobey, 184
Maine, 264, 290
Mall of America, 78, 268
Mallon, Meg, 10
Malls, 78
Malone, Karl, 19
Malone, Moses, 19
Mammals, 105–109
Manila, 147
Manning, Peyton, 42
Mansion at the MGM Grand,
    207
Mantle, Mickey, 28
Maple syrup, 290
Marabou stork, 98
Mardi Gras, 246
Marino, Dan, 35
Maris, Roger, 211
Mars, 223, 225, 226, 232
Martin, Curtis, 36
Maryland, 265
Massachusetts, 266
Mays, Willie, 23
McCartney, Paul, 173, 175

McDonald's, 201
McGwire, Mark, 22, 211
McLaren F1, 239
Mears, Rick, 67
Meat, 144
Merckx, Eddy, 7
Mercury, 225, 226, 232
Metro, 72
Mexican, The, 191
Mexico, 88, 140, 141, 154
Mexico City, 72
Miami Dolphins, 43
Michigan, 267
Mickelson, Phil, 9
Microsoft, 203
Middleton Place Gardens, 285
Midler, Bette, 174
MiG-25 Foxbat, 243
Migration, 100, 123
Milky Way, 231
Millennium Dome, 82
Miller Outdoor Theater, 270
Minnesota, 268
Mississippi, 254, 269
Mississippi Sports Hall of Fame, 255
Mississippi-Missouri River, 128
Missouri, 270
Mittal, Lakshmi, 203
Mona Lisa Smile, 191
Monarch butterfly, 123
Monet, Claude, 194
Monster trucks, 241
Montana, 271
Montoya, Juan-Pablo, 67
Montreal Canadiens, 62
Moon, Warren, 35
Moons, 223, 229
Moose, 110
Morceli, Noureddine, 6
Moscow, 71, 72
Motorcycles, 236
Mount Baker, 145
Mount Copeland, 145
Mount Everest, 124
Mount Kea, 256
Mount Rainier, 145
Mount Washington, 150
Mountain Dell Dam, 281
Mountains, 124, 131
Movie theaters, 187

Movies, 182–192
MSN, 214
Multiple arch dams, 281
Municipal Theater, 270
Murphy, Eddie, 182
Mushrooms, 156
Musial, Stan, 25, 29, 33
Music, 171–179
Musicians, 171–179

Nabisco, 258
NASA, 243
National forests, 247
National sites, 90
Navratilova, Martina, 44, 46
Nebraska, 272
Nemcova, Eva, 18
Neptune, 223, 227, 228, 230
Nests, 101
Nevada, 273
New England Patriots, 43
New Guinea, 132
New Hampshire, 150, 274, 290
New Jersey, 275
New Mexico, 276
New Orleans, 150
New York, 71, 72, 290
New York Botanical Gardens, 285
New York City, 72, 80, 86
New York Yankees, 30, 251
New Zealand, 139, 143, 186
Ngeny, Noah, 6
Nicklaus, Jack, 11
Nile River, 128
Nintendo, 235
Nissan Altima, 196
Noah's Ark, 294
Nocturnal animal exhibits, 272
North Carolina, 278
North Dakota, 279
North Island, 207
Norway, 75, 141, 205
Nozomi train, 238
Nunavut, 134

O'Neal, Shaquille, 17
Oakland Athletics, 30
Oceans, 130
Office buildings, 291
Oh! Calcutta!, 181

Ohio, 260, 280
Oil spills, 163
Ojos del Salado, 125
Oklahoma, 281
Oklahoma City, 164
Olympics, 50–57
Onassis Roussel, Athina, 206
Oranges, 136
Orbits, 226
Oregon, 282
Orinoco River, 129
Oruro, 76
Oscars (see Academy Awards®)
Ostrich, 102, 103
Ostrov Bol'shoy, 146
Our Family Trouble, 191

Pacarana, 107
Pacific Ocean, 130
Pagani Zonda C1257.3, 212
Page Field, 265
Page, Larry, 206
Paintings, 194
Paradise Station, 145
Paris, 71, 86, 87
Park at MOA, The, 268
Parmigiani Fleurier Toric Corrector Quantième Perpétual, 208
Parthenon at Mt. Olympus, The, 268
Patterson, James, 193
Payton, Walter, 36
Pennsylvania, 260, 283, 290
Pensacola Dam, 281
Pentagon, 291
Peregrine falcon, 99
Perenty, 118
Peru, 133
Petermann's Kunststuben, 210
Petersen, William, 168
Petrified wood, 286
Petronas Twin Towers, 83
Phantom of the Opera, The, 181
Phelps, Michael, 57
Philbin, Regis, 170
Philippines, 134, 222
Picasso, Pablo, 194
Pig, 108
Pinglin Highway Tunnel, 75
Pink Floyd, 175

Pittsburgh Steelers, 40
Pizza Hut, 201
Plains Viscacha, 107
Planes, 243
Plants, 151–159
Player, Gary, 11
Plushchenko, Yevgeny, 49
Pluto, 229, 230, 232
Point Barrow, 146
Poison, 114, 115, 156, 158
Poison dart frog, 112
Polar Express, The, 188
Pollution, 163
Porsche Carrera GT, 212
Post offices, 274
Potato chips, 139
Potosi, 76
Presley, Elvis, 171, 176
Producers (movie), 189
Producers, The, 180
Pronghorn antelope, 109
Proxima Centauri, 224
Pumpkins, 253

Q1, 81
Queen Mary 2, 240
Quibdo, 148

Raffia palm, 152
Rafflesia, 157
Rahal, Bobby, 67
Rain forest, 112, 133
Rainfall, 148
Ramirez, Manny, 26
Red king crab, 92
Red knot, 100
Redding (CA), 248
Renoir, Pierre Auguste, 194
Reptiles, 113–115, 118–119
Resolute, 146
Restaurants, 201, 210
Retail stores, 249
Reticulated python, 113
Rhino, 110
Rhode Island, 284
Rice, Jerry, 37
Ricin, 158
Riggins, John, 38
Ripken, Jr., Cal, 32, 34
Rivers, 129
Roadrunner, 103
Roads, 73
Roberston Airport, 265

Roberts, Julia, 191
Roberts, Nora, 193
Robots, 219
Rochester (MN), 261
Rocky Mountains, 131
Rodents, 107
Rodriguez, Alex, 26, 28
Roger Dubuis Excalibur EX
    08, 208
Roller coasters, 244
Rolling Stones, The, 178
Ronaldo, Cristiano, 60
Rose, Pete, 25, 27, 32
Rowling, J.K., 193
Roy, Patrick, 64
Royal Gorge Bridge, 84
Rush Hour 2, 190
Russia, 88, 134
Ruth, Babe, 23, 27, 33
Ryan, Nolan, 24

Sagittarius Dwarf, 234
Saguaro cactus, 153
Sahara Desert, 127
Sailfest, 262
Sailfish, 97
Saint Peter's Basilica, 82
Salary, 168, 169
Saleen S7, 212, 239
Salina (KS), 253
Salmon pink birdeater, 120
Saltwater crocodile, 119
Sampras, Pete, 45, 47
San Francisco 49ers, 40
San Francisco Giants, 30
Sanchez-Vicario, Aranxta, 44
Sanders, Barry, 36
Saturn, 223, 227–229
Schmidt, Mike, 29
Schwarzenegger, Arnold, 190
Scott, Everett, 34
Scottsdale (AZ), 248
Sculptures, 279
Sea horse, 96
Seabreeze Park, 252
Sears Roebuck, 249
Sears Tower, 83, 291
Second Star of Africa, 135
Seeds, 159
Seikan Tunnel, 74
Semel, Terry, 197
Seoul, 72
Seychelles, 159

Shanghai, 80
Shankweiler's Drive-In
    Theater, 283
Sharks, 104
Shea Stadium, 266
Sheindlin, Judge Judy, 170
Shin-Kanmon Tunnel, 74
Ship canals, 77
Shrek 2, 183, 184
Shula, Don, 41
Sichuan Province, 76
Silver Bullet, 242
Sinatra, Frank, 176
Singapore, 147, 186
Singers (see musicians)
Singh, Vijay, 9
Singita Private Game Reserve,
    207
Sinise, Gary, 168
Six Flags Great Adventure,
    79, 244
Sketch, 210
Skiing, 54, 55
Skowhegan State Fair, 264
Skyscrapers, 80
Slate red ornamental, 120
Slim Helú, Carlos, 203
Sloth, 108
Small Magellanic Cloud, 231,
    234
SMART-1, 242
Smith, Emmitt, 36–38
Smith, Katie, 21
Smith, Will, 190
Snakes, 114, 115
*Snow White and the Seven
    Dwarfs,* 183
Snowfall, 145
Soccer, 58–61
Sociable weaver, 101
Soda, 141
Soft drinks, 141
Somalia, 204
Sopranos, The, 168
Sorenstam, Annika, 8, 10
Sosa, Sammy, 22, 23, 211
South America, 133
South Carolina, 263, 285
South China Mall, 78
South Dakota, 286
South Korea, 219
South Pole, 150
Soybeans, 137

Space walks, 233
Spain, 87, 140, 144
Spas, 293
Speaker, Tris, 25
Sperm whale, 93, 105
Spider-Man, 184
Spiders, 120
Spielberg, Steven, 189
Spine-tailed swift, 99
Spirit of America, 237
Sports Halls of Fame, 255
Springsteen, Bruce, 171
St. Gotthard Tunnel, 75
St. Lawrence, 77
St. Louis Cardinals, 30
Stanford University, 12
Stanley Cup, 62
Star Wars, 182, 209
*Star Wars: Episode III—
   Revenge of the Sith*, 184
*Star Wars: Episode I—The
   Phantom Menace*, 192
Starlight Theater, 270
Stars, 224
State fairs, 264
Stefani, Gwen, 174
Storebaelt, 85
Streisand, Barbra, 172
Strobl, Fritz, 55
Suárez, Claudio, 58
Submillimeter Wavelength
   Telescope, 256
Subway (sandwich shop),
   201
Subway systems, 71, 72
Sugar beets, 137
Sugar cane, 137
Sumatra, 157
Sunflower, 157
Super Bowl, 40
Super Mario Bros. 3, 235
Super Mario Kart, 235
Super Mario Land 2, 235
Supercomputers, 216
Superdome, 82
Survivor, 241
Suzuki GSX1300R
   Hayabusa, 236
Swainson's hawk, 100
Sweden, 143, 218
Sweet potato, 137
Swimming, 52, 53
Switzerland, 142, 205

Swoopes, Sheryl, 21

Tacoma Narrows, 84
Taipan, 115
Taipei 101, 83
Taiwan, 83
Talk shows, 170
Tanzania, 204
Target, 249
Tarkenton, Frank, 35
Tarzan, 188
Television, 167–170, 222
Temperature, 146–150
Temples, 284
Tennessee Aquarium, 287
Tennessee, 287
Tennis, 44–47
Terminator 3, 190
Texas, 246, 254, 263, 269,
   288
Texas Star, 288
TGV train, 238
Thailand, 147, 222
Theme parks, 252, 268
Thompson Pass, 145
Thompson, Tina, 21
Thompson's gazelle, 109
Thoroughly Modern Millie,
   180
Thouot, Pierre, 233
Thrust 2, 237
Thrust SSC, 237
Thunder Over Louisville, 262
Thunderbird, 216
Tidal waves, 160
Tijuana, 86
Time Warner Network, 214
Tipas, 125
Titan, 229
Titanic, 185, 192
Toiyabe National Forest, 247
Tokyo, 71, 72, 80
Tokyo Bay Aqualine, 74
Tomato, 136
Tongass National Forest, 247
Tonto National Forest, 247
Tony Awards, 180
Top Thrill Dragster, 244
Tornado (plane), 243
Tornadoes, 164
Tornikidou, Elena, 18
Toronto Maple Leafs, 65
Tour de l'Ile, 208

Tourism, 86, 87
Touro Synagogue, 284
Tower of Terror, 244
Toyota Camry, 196
Toyota Corolla, 196
Toys, 199
Traffic, 70, 73
Trains, 238, 292
Transatlantic Mountains, 131
Transportation, 70–73
Travel, 86–90
Treasure Planet, 188
Trees, 152, 155
Tregunter Tower III, 81
Triangulum Galaxy, 231
Tropical forests, 133
Trump, Donald, 168
Trump Tower, 267
Trump World Towers, 81
Trumpeter swan, 98
Tsunamis, 160
Tucker, Chris, 190
Tunnels, 74, 75, 277, 292
Turkey, 222
Turtles, 117
Twain, Shania, 174
Twins Day Festival, 280
Two International Finance
   Centre, 83

U2, 178
UCLA, 13
UK, 139, 142, 199, 221
United Arab Emirates, 138
United Health Group, 197
United States, 70, 73, 87, 88,
   139, 141, 143, 144, 154,
   186, 187, 199, 205, 215,
   218, 219, 221
United Technologies, 197
Universities, 278
University of Connecticut, 12
University of Georgia, 278
University of North Carolina,
   278
University of Vermont, 278
Uranus, 223, 227–229, 230
Uruguay, 59
Utah, 289

Van den Hoogenband, Pieter,
   52
Vacheron Constantin, 208

Valdez, 150
Vegetables, 137, 138
Venus, 225, 226, 232
Vermont, 290
Verrazano-Narrows, 84
Viaduc de Millau, 84
Vick, Michael, 42
Video games, 235
Viewers, 167
Virginia, 291
Virginia Sports Hall of Fame, 255
Volcanoes, 125
Von Thurn und Taxis, Albert, 206
Voss, James, 233
Voyager of the Seas, 240

Wadi Halfa, 149
Waialeale, 148
Wal-Mart, 217, 249
Walton, Alice, 202
Walton, Christy, 202
Walton, Helen, 202
Ward Pound Ridge
  Reservation, 271
Warwick, Dionne, 177

Washington, 145, 292
Washington Redskins, 40
Watches, 208
Water monitor, 118
Water parks, 294
Waterfalls, 267
Watermelon, 136
Wealth, 202–206
Weather, 145–150
Web sites, 214
Webb, Karrie, 10
Weeds, 151
Wenchuan, 76
West Edmonton Mall, 78
West Indian butterfly, 121
West Side Story, 185
West, Jerry, 15
West Virginia, 293
Whales, 105
White Mountains, 150
White rhino, 106
White-rumped sandpiper, 100
Whooper swan, 98
Wild turkey, 103
Williams, Billy, 34
Wills-Moody, Helen, 46
Wind, 150, 165

Winfrey, Oprah, 170
Wingspan, 98
Wisconsin, 294
Wisconsin Dells, 294
Witherspoon, Reese, 191
Witt, Katarina, 48
Woods, Tiger, 9, 11
Woodstock Fair, 264
World Cup (soccer), 59
Wrigley Field, 266
Wyoming, 295

X-43A, 243

Yagudin, Alexei, 49
Yahoo!, 197, 214
Yangtze River, 128, 129, 162
Yankee Stadium, 266
Yastrzemski, Carl, 32
Yellow-billed cuckoo, 103
Yellowfin tuna, 97
Yenisei River, 128
York (PA), 253
Yuma (AZ), 248

Zaire River, 129
Zidane, Zinedine, 60

WILD WACKY AND AMAZING FACTS

Animals • Movies • Music
Sports • Television
Food • Technology

Snuggle with a Puggle

The echidna and the platypus are the only two mammals in the world that lay eggs. Part of the family of animals known as monotremes, the echidna lays one grape-sized egg a year and stores it in its pouch for 10 days. The egg then hatches, and the baby—known as a puggle—is about the size of a jelly bean. The puggle remains in its mother's pouch for about 50 days and drinks milk that the mother secretes in her pouch. The puggle then moves into the mother's burrow, and eventually hunts on its own when it's about seven months old.

The nest belonging to a colony of sociable weavers can measure 20 feet (6.1 m) wide and 10 feet (3 m) tall. This massive home can contain more than 100 nesting chambers and weigh several tons. Some of these nests are used by several sociable weaver generations for more than a century, with up to 400 birds calling the nest home at any one time.

No-Nonsense Nest

Furry Seafood

In 2006, divers announced that they had discovered a new crustacean in the South Pacific near Easter Island in about 7,540 feet (1,500 km) of water. The crustacean measures about 6 inches (15 cm) long, and its claws are covered with soft, blond hair. The furry little lobster is called Kiwa hirsute. It is so unusual, it was given its own family and genus.

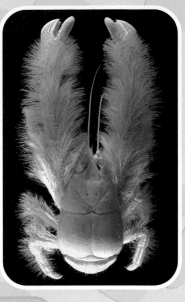

Larva Lunch

The larva of the Polyphemus moth of North America is hungry! In its first two days of life, it can consume a quantity of food equivalent to 86,000 times its own body weight. That's about the equivalent of a 7-pound (3.1 kg) baby eating 270 tons (245 t) of food during the same period!

Breakfast with a Boa

Boa constrictors are talented ambush hunters on the ground, but these sneaky snakes can also hunt in the air. Boas wait up in the trees until they sense a bat approaching, and then knock it out of the air as it flies by. Once prey has been stunned, the boa wraps its body around its prey until it suffocates. The meal is then swallowed whole.

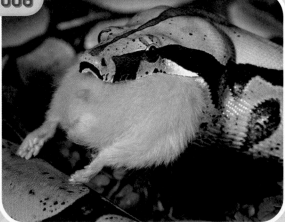

Building Blocks

The seemingly colossal New York set of *King Kong* (2005) was actually only four blocks long and one story high. The rest of the set was added digitally, and more than 90,000 different buildings were created by computer. Streets were also extended using digital effects, and the number of pedestrians and cars were doubled or even tripled in large scenes.

The Batmobile measures 9 feet (2.7 m) wide and 16 feet (4.9 m) long, and can cruise along at a top speed of 106 miles (171 k) per hour. And when Batman really needs to fly, it can accelerate from 0 to 60 miles (96.6 k) per hour in just six seconds. The car sports a 5.7-liter V8 Chevy engine and runs on unleaded gas. The Batmobile was designed in England and is worth about $595,000.

Crime-Fighting Car

Silly Stand-In

Yoda has been part of the Star Wars movies for years, but he has been digitally created since *Star Wars: Episode II—Attack of the Clones* in 2002. While filming *Star Wars: Episode III—Revenge of the Sith* in 2005, the producers thought it would be easier for the actors if one of the old Yoda puppets was used as a reference point. The puppet they found, however, had not been stored very well, and its face had melted into a very funny expression. Although the puppet did help block out the scene, it was hard for the actors not to laugh at the twisted Yoda peering back at them.

More than 206,563 gallons (781,926 l) of fake chocolate were made for the river area in *Charlie and the Chocolate Factory*. Another 38,430 gallons (145,473 l) of it were made for the waterfall. The lollipops on the trees, the giant pink candy canes, and the giant humbugs were real candy. While Nestlé provided 1,850 bars of real chocolate for the movie, another 110,000 plastic bars were made and wrapped by the company.

Candy Creations

While filming *The Chronicles of Narnia: The Lion, the Witch and the Wardrobe*, producers had to ask permission to bring 12 reindeer into New Zealand to pull the Ice Queen's sled. The Ministry of Agriculture and Forestry denied the request due to a fear of introducing a disease to the country's livestock. However, eight wolves were allowed into the country, and they pulled the sled instead.

Bring in the Wolves

How Original

The song title "Angel" has made it into the Top 40 twelve times—more than any other song title. Each time it appeared, it was as a completely different song by a different artist. The singers to score big with their "Angel" song include Rod Stewart (1972), Aretha Franklin (1973), Madonna (1985), Eurythmics (1990), Jon Secada (1993), Massive Attack (1998), Ralph Fridge (2000), Lionel Richie (2000), Shaggy (2001), Sarah McLachlan (2002), the Corrs (2004), and Pharrell Williams (2006).

Music by the Megabyte

A total of 332.7 million music tracks were downloaded off of the Internet in 2005—an increase of 148% from the previous year. In fact, the biggest downloading week in history occurred between Christmas and New Year's Eve 2005, with more than 9.6 million tracks sold. iTunes accounts for about 70% of the download market, and outsells many traditional music stores, including Tower Records, Borders, and Sam Goody. The music download industry made $1.1 billion dollars for the year.

Grade-A Goody Bag

Presenters at the MTV Video Music Awards not only get to attend a rocking party, they get a giant gift bag with $27,000 worth of cool stuff inside. Some of the goodies inside the 2005 denim Gap Weekender bag included a Caribbean resort vacation, an iPod shuffle, Missoni sunglasses, a Dooney & Bourke duffle bag, a 24-karat gold eye-lash curler, a collection of designer T-shirts, and an unlimited supply of Nestlé/Wonka candy for one year.

Success by the Numbers

Paul McCartney is the only musician to top the charts as a solo artist, as well as part of a duo, trio, quartet, and quintet. As a solo artist, "Pipes of Peace" reached number one in 1982. As part of a duo with Stevie Wonder, McCartney saw number one with "Ebony and Ivory," also in 1982. As part of the trio Wings, he reached number one in 1977 with "Mull of Kintyre." He had 16 chart-toppers between 1963 and 1969 as one of the four members of The Beatles. And, also in 1969, The Beatles joined with Billy Preston for the song "Get Back," which made it all the way to number one as well.

Chart Hog

In 2004, Nelly had two of his albums—*Suit* and *Sweat*—debut as numbers one and two on the Billboard 200 chart. He's the first solo artist in history to have two records debut in the two highest spots simultaneously. *Suit*—featuring the hit single "My Place"—sold 396,000 copies during its first week, while *Sweat*—driven by the popular single "Flap Your Wings"—sold 342,000 copies.

Look Out!

MLB player Ron Hunt must have been a sore man—he holds three different records for being hit by pitches. He was hit by a pitch the most times in one game (3), the most times in a season (50), and the most times in a career (243). Hunt played 1,483 games in his MLB career, so on average, he got beaned with a ball every sixteenth game.

Third Time's a Charm

Joe Montana is the only football player to be named Super Bowl MVP three times. As a quarterback for the San Francisco 49ers, Montana earned these awards in Super Bowl XVI (1982), Super Bowl XIX (1985) and Super Bowl XXIV (1990). Joe Cool—as he came to be known—retired from football in 1994 and was inducted into the Pro Football Hall of Fame in 2000.

During the 17 days of the 2006 Winter Olympics in Torino, Italy, a total of 84 medals were awarded to the best of the 2,500 competing athletes from 80 different countries. There were 650 judges watching over the seven different sports, including biathlon, bobsledding, curling, ice hockey, luge, skating, and skiing. Approximately 26,000 volunteers helped to make the Games a success, and some 10,000 members of the media kept the fans updated.

Olympic Overview

Super Speedy Stat

NASCAR legend Bill Elliot holds the record for fastest lap speed in a stock car. In 1987, he raced around the 2.66-mile (4.3 km) Talledega International Speedway during the Daytona 500 at 212.8 miles (342.5 k) per hour! If he had been able to maintain that speed, he could have driven from New York City to Los Angeles in just 13 hours!

B-Ball Banter

A few NBA players have ended up with some pretty unusual nicknames. For instance, Allen Iverson of the Philadelphia 76ers is called The Answer because he became the team's leading scorer soon after being drafted. Shawn Marion of the Phoenix Suns is known as The Matrix because of his gravity-defying moves. Marion's teammate Amare Stoudemire is called STAT, which means Standing Tall and Talented. And LA Laker Kobe Bryant is called The Mamba because his highly accurate shots are similar to the snake's precise striking ability.

Plane and Simple

The airplane wreckage featured on *Lost* is a very important part of the show. Before filming began, ABC decided not to fly the plane out to the set in Hawaii. They sent a team of production assistants to choose the pieces they wanted as the plane was being dismantled in Mojave, California. Pieces of the retired Lockheed Tristar plane were then flown to Hawaii and strategically placed throughout the set. Before starring in a hit TV drama, the aircraft flew for 26 years and accumulated 58,841 flight hours.

No Diving Allowed!

On Fox's *The OC,* the Cohen's pool looks normal, but it is only 4 feet (1.2 m) deep. This could pose a problem, since some of the cast is fairly tall—Adam Brody (Seth) is 5'11" (1.8 m), and Peter Gallagher (Sandy), Benjamin McKenzie (Ryan), and Mischa Barton (Marissa) are 5'9" (1.7 m). To make it look more realistic, the cast has to do the pool scenes on their knees.

A State of Science

CSI: Crime Scene Investigation is set in Las Vegas because that city has the second-most-active crime lab in the country (beaten only by the FBI lab at Quantico, Virginia). To keep things as realistic as possible, all the equipment in the television show's lab is fully functional. It was either purchased by the show or donated by manufacturers.

Food Fears

All food items eaten on *Fear Factor* must be approved by the U.S. Department of Agriculture before being featured on the show. Some of these tasty treats are also tested by *Fear Factor* production assistants. If the assistants complete the stunt, they earn $100. Some past *Fear Factor* snacks have included camel spiders, rotten milk, sheep eyes, and live cockroaches.

On *24*, each episode represents one hour of one day, eventually showing a full day spread out over the entire TV season. To keep all of the actors looking the same as they did the episode before, cast members are required to have their hair trimmed every five days.

Just a Little Off the Top

Super Spud Stats

Potatoes are the second-most-consumed food in the United States—only dairy products are eaten more than these tasty vegetables. The average American eats about 140 pounds (63.5 kg) of this starchy staple per year. That's about 10,500 pounds (4,763 kg) of potatoes in a lifetime—almost the same weight as a small elephant. Some 16 pounds (7.3 kg) are eaten in the form of french fries, and another 7 pounds (3.2 kg) are in the form of crisps and chips.

Packed with Prizes

A ball game favorite since 1896, Cracker Jack offers hungry snackers more than peanuts and caramel-coated popcorn. To date, consumers have found more than 23 billion toy surprises inside their snack boxes. In fact, Cracker Jack gives out more promotional toys than any other company. And some of those toys are quite valuable. A series of baseball cards that were included in some 1915 Cracker Jack boxes are worth $60,000 today.

Accidentally Delicious

Although the tortilla chip is now one of the country's favorite snack foods, it started off as a mistake. Rebecca Webb Carranza, co-owner of a tortilla factory in Los Angeles, was looking for a way to salvage odd-shaped tortillas that were rejected from the tortilla manufacturing machines. She cut up the tortillas, fried them, and sold them for a dime a bag in her Mexican deli. The crispy chips were a hit, and today Americans spend almost $2 billion on them annually.

One Cool Customer

Kool-Aid—the fruit-flavored drink that's been quenching kids' thirst since 1927—has a well-dressed spokesman called the Kool-Aid Man. The juicy mascot is always dressed according to the flavor of the package he appears on. For instance, Kool-Aid Man wears a bathing suit and flip-flops on the Island Twist flavors; skis and earmuffs on Kool Pops; and fatigues and combat boots on packages sold on military bases. Each year, more than 563 million gallons of Kool-Aid are consumed.

Each day, Hershey's produces 80 million of their Kisses at their Pennsylvania and California factories. That equals 29.2 billion Kisses each year. Once the little candies are formed, machines can wrap foil around 1,300 of the tasty treats every minute. It takes 99 of these little Kisses to make up a pound (.5 kg) of chocolate. To ensure that Hershey's can keep churning out Kisses each day, the Pennsylvania factory stores about 90 million pounds (40.8 million kg) of cocoa beans—enough to make approximately 102.1 billion kisses.

Creating the Kisses

The LifeStraw™ is a water purification device that filters out harmful bacteria and debris, making normally undrinkable water safe to consume. The straw contains a special material that kills germs on contact, and this can prevent ingesting bacteria that cause illnesses such as typhoid. The straw, which was introduced in 2006, costs just $3 and will last for about a year.

Water Water Everywhere

Tuning in to TV

Now there is even less that can come between TV viewers and their favorite programs. The Slingbox—a little device that hooks up to a viewer's home television set—can send any shows available on that set to any other device connected to the Internet. For instance, a New Yorker on vacation in Paris can watch his local news on his cell phone. Viewers can even watch a show recorded on their TiVo, or tune into a DVD that someone at home is currently watching.

On A Roll

For those looking for an alternative to in-line skates, the new LandRollers might just be the answer. Using two larger wheels on the outside of each foot, these skates don't look like anything seen before. The skater's weight offsets the wheels' tilt, making it easier for even beginning users to remain balanced. And even experts are taking notice— Olympic speed skating gold medalist Apolo Anton Ohno just signed on as a spokesperson.

Aspiring Architects

For budding architects who need to build their own designs today, LEGO® may be able to help out. The company now has software that lets builders plan their own creation and submit it to LEGO®. LEGO® will then determine which bricks are needed and create a kit just for that design. Just like any other blueprints, the price depends on the complexity of the project.

Food at Your Fingertips

Students may never have to remember their lunch money again. School cafeterias can install machines that will scan students' fingerprints and use them to access debit accounts holding lunch money. Called the iMeal, the scanner recognizes 40 points on the fingertip, and pulls the student's record. And once the food is scanned, it can also alert the cashier if the student is allergic to any of the food he or she has chosen.